A novel

Judith C. Owens-Lalude

DUNKER
AnikePress
Worldwide Publisher
Henderson, Nevada, USA

Revised 2023, © copyright 2016

Orders:
www.AnikePress.com
www.Amazon.com

ISBN: 978-0-9863672-3-6
LCCN: 2016901493

Discussion questions
Event photographs from the Owens-Lalude album

Book cover design, illustrations, and layout
by Judith C. Owens-Lalude

To contact the author or receive information
about book signings and related programs:
http://jcamilleculturalacademy.com
jclalude@gmail.com

All rights reserved. No part of this book may be reproduced in any form by electronic or mechanical means (including photocopying, recording, or information storage and retrieval) without permission in writing from the publisher, except by a reviewer, who might include brief quotations in a review. Copyright 2016, Judith C. Owens-Lalude, Louisville, Kentucky.

DUNKER is Dedicated to:
My loving husband, A. O'tayo Lalude M.D.,
and my two, always-supportive, sons
A. Adesina Lalude and Akinwande A. Lalude

Along with:
Students from around the world who want to know
more about American teenagers,
American teenagers who never made it to their high school
proms, students who need a read written just for them,
middle school students looking ahead, and
moms and dads looking back.

TABLE OF CONTENTS

1	School Bells	1
2	Pass the Ball	25
3	Big Blue and a Black Eye	37
4	Dunker Scores	60
5	Paper Dolls	76
6	Uptown	83
7	Two Points	103
8	Barbershop Blues	114
9	If the Shoe Fits	132
10	Timeout	156
11	The Dance Lesson	166
12	Pretty in Pink	171
13	Dribble and Drive	194
14	The Overlook	213
15	The All-night Party	218
16	Dunker's Home	224
	Discussion Questions	232
	About the Author	235
	Alfred "Butch" Beard	237
	Other Books	238

1

School Bells
Dunker

I flipped my top, trapping cool air against my gut. The school bus doors sprang open. My heart leaped as my neck brushed against the damp collar of my shirt. When my eyes blinked, a gush of students fast-tracked through my space, except Mariah. Not taking my eyes off the predators, I inched through the noisy pack, still not seeing her. We needed to talk. This prom's crawling up my back like Coach Ben on a bad practice day, and Mr. Drew's barking unreasonable to-do Physics assignments didn't help my situation.

Before I knew it, the crowd had dragged my body backward, plastering me against one of the double doors that opened to a massive hallway. I was a six-foot-tall stranger in my own schoolyard.

"Man! You okay?"

I didn't see Sly until his voice clawed at my nerves. At 6 feet 3 inches, he was the tallest on the basketball team, played the center position, and was the captain. He stood close to me to talk, too close. He made me feel so uneasy, I wanted to spit at him, but Grandma's voice sounded off in my head. "A gentleman, never, ever spits at another person," it said.

Sly put his hand on my shoulder and rocked it like he was trying to jar me from a butt-kicking nightmare.

"I'm cool, man. Take your ball-palming hand off of my shoulder and move your tight ass on down the hallway."

I turned my focus back to the crowd. Why Sly couldn't find another door to enter, just this one day, I didn't know.

"Check you later, man," Sly said.

His big feet did a one-two step. He caught up with the cheerleaders who squealed his name, the same as they did on game nights when he dribbled the ball downcourt for a fancy layup shot. He grabbed one of them by the arm. I was history, and that was a good thing. I didn't have time for Sly's jive.

"Gee whiz!" I said to myself.

Here comes Jake with his lanky self. He invaded my space before I had time to recover from Sly's pesky visit.

The dude wore a buttoned-up cardigan and high-water pants held in place by suspenders. The cuffs rode above his ankles, further up than they needed to be. They say Jake's gonna be voted the Best-Dressed Senior Boy. I'm not sure about that. With his cool dressing, he turned a lot of heads of guys and girls, but not mine.

"Hey, man, what's up with you? Ya smirking and doing that side-to-side rock. Nervous or something?" Jake asked.

I drew my lips tight to dismiss him, but it didn't work. He continued barking annoyances at me.

"Hey, Dude! Relax. You look tight. Open your mouth. Let it out. I want to hear about what's got you in such a way."

Judith C. Owens-Lalude

Jake didn't know what he was asking me to do. If only I could sit him next to Grandma for a serious chat. She'd give him an oversized load of shit about necking on the front porch, keeping his hands from underneath a girl's skirt, and minding his manners.

"I'm tight. Now split, or I'm gonna pretend you're high weeds in my backyard and sickle you down until you can play ball with the grasshoppers."

Jake gave me a hefty shoulder-to-shoulder basketball nudge. "See you later man," he said and did a jock's long step down the hallway with a bouncy jock's gait and his head bobbing above everyone else's. I supposed he was on his way to someplace special. I didn't know where to this early in the morning–to meet up with girls, I'd guess.

Just as I got back to studying the herd, the Bender twins, Darryl and Darnell, swaggered into my domain uninvited and grinning.

"You sick, Dunker?" they chimed with an identical singsong pitch.

"Yeah! Step aside, or I'll up-chuck a double dose of matching puke on the two of you."

"Chill, man," they warned and faded into the mob.

I glanced over my shoulder when coolness airbrushed my arm. Mr. Belkin, the new janitor, was closing the door I leaned against. When both of them were open, a magnificent wind tunnel was created in the corridor. It reminded me of the ones we studied in Physics class.

I abandoned my post and sauntered down the hallway. I'd squandered too much time searching for Mariah on the schoolyard. Luckily, I didn't have to stop at my locker on my way to Civics class–a special session being held in the library today.

Moving on, I collided with hot bodies emitting fragrances from scented soaps, after-shaves, and perfumes that mingled and fought to consume the air around me.

I was glad I didn't have to go to my usual first-period English class, although, I was anxious about my Civics homework. Feeling ready to present my paper, I sat at the library table and waited my turn at the podium and hoped nothing dumb would come out of my mouth when it was my turn to speak. Being surrounded by books, globes, maps and shelves made the environment feel a little strange. Today, we were characters, politicians, or civil rights leaders from the past.

After several presentations, Mrs. Shelby said, "Mr. Womack, You'll be next."

I got up and stood in front of my classmates. After Max, who presented before me sat down, I approached the podium and opened my black binder with the paper titled *Civil Rights and the Vote* clipped inside. All eyes were on me as I read and didn't fumble once.

"Mr. Womack, you won't need to do the extra assignment for your final grade. You have met all the requirements for this class."

Back in the hallway, I was giddy with delight and wished I could tell Mariah about the good news.

I slid my hand into my pocket and leaned to balance the weight of my satchel that cut into my shoulder. If only Mariah and I could be put on the timeout bench together. Sitting there alone, we'd talk things over. The prom was at the top of the list followed by school, grades, college, scholarships, and, oh yes, basketball.

Time itself had worked its way to the top of my priority list. It was out of control and slipping by too fast. I needed to fast freeze it.

Hanukkah had passed and Christmas, too. Valentine's Day was history. That's the day I sat the chocolate heart I had bought for Mariah on Big Blue's hood, forgetting he overheated at times. The candy melted. Just as well, since I couldn't get next to Mariah that day anyway. Time fast-forwarded 'til shamrocks papered the locker doors.

Next, I was boiling eggs on Easter Eve. I wanted to write I Love You *on one of them, but I didn't want the whole world to know how I felt. Instead, I pushed the wax pencil along, etching* M-A-R-I-A-H *on them. I balanced one of the eggs on a spoon and eased it into a dark, red dye. Zap! Big, bright, white letters glimmered below the red surface. Mariah's translucent face floated over them. She stared at me. My eyes boogied. My knees wobbled.*

Judith C. Owens-Lalude

Minutes stretched out triple time. My mouth was dry and open. I wasn't able to speak.

I raised the egg, shifted my belt buckle with my left hand, and tilted the spoon with my right hand. The egg rolled onto a kitchen towel. The stark white fibers snatched the droplets that fired off beet-red rays. Had my heart just exploded? Enough of this.

I shook my head to clear my mind as I made my way to second-period Calculus class with Mr. Simmons. At the end of the class period, he told us we would review applications and the development of probability tomorrow. That meant the time would pass quickly. It always did when he lectured to us. Today, it seemed we were in and out of class in record time.

I was back in the hallway and on my way to Physics. For some reason, Sly and the two-of-a-kind twins crept into my thoughts. The cheerleaders always said Darryl and Darnell were cute. The only difference between the two of them and the rest of us was that they were carbon copies of each other. They walked the same pigeon-toed walk; shook hands with the same cold, damp, but firm grip; and their grins were mirror images–even their teeth. On the other hand, they resembled the rest of the players on the team: too tall, too lean, with feet too big. Nonetheless, they were true jocks and played good ball. Betcha, if I stomped on the toe of one of them, his twin would holler ouch. Maybe I could turn Toby, my nine-year-old brother, into my twin and get someone to stomp on my toe.

"Hehehe!" I chuckled as I turned the corner. I rose off my heels at the sight of Mariah. "Ooo-wee," I whistled from underneath my breath. A fire lit itself beneath my feet. Heat rushed up my legs to my eyeballs. I slapped both my jaws and mumbled, "Good Lord, if I were a white man, I'd be blood-red!"

I grabbed hold of my satchel and pushed my way through the crowd. My heart galloped along with my feet. I worked my way down the hall, sucking in massive gulps of air to downshift my heartbeat. It didn't work. I let it rip. When I got closer to Mariah, I backstepped to keep from plowing into her. I stopped inches from her body. I eased my right foot next to her left and rested my palm on her locker's frame which cooled its festering flesh.

When I narrowed the gap between us, my lips reached for her jaw. I was falling in love with the left side of Mariah's face.

In the lowest tone possible, not wanting neighboring ears to decipher my words in case I fumbled, bit my tongue, or made a fool of myself, I said, "Hey, girl. What's up?" When the words came out, they had the sound of squeaky hinges on a haunted house. Disgust coated me like talcum on a baby's bottom.

"Not much, Dunker."

My teammates nicknamed me Dunker because I can get underneath the basketball net, come straight up off the floor, damn near three feet, and slam-dunk the ball. *Pill* we call it.

"How's your game?" Mariah asked.

She didn't know *talking game* made my hand itch. Without a command, it went up to catch the pill that wasn't there. When it did, my book satchel slipped off my shoulder. It tilted me over, so close to Mariah that only goosebumps separated us.

DUNKER

"Dunker!"

I snapped with basketball-practice precision when she called my name.

"Dunker," Mariah said a second time.

The songbird's voice allured me away from my imaginary center court. I examined Mariah's eyes for a micro bit of reassurance. What I saw restructured my confidence, somewhat.

"I ah. I ah. Just wanted to . . . "

The gap between us vanished. We were flesh-to-flesh with no goosebumps between us. I shriveled into a mass of wimpish agar only fit for a Petri dish.

"Mariah!" the girlfriends called.

Searching for the source of the voices, Mariah blocked me with the back of her head. I opened my mouth to snatch back her attention. When I reached for her, my half-zipped bag burped up an avalanche of papers and composition notebooks that flooded the purple and green floor beneath my feet. At the speed of a slam dunk, I was down on my knee, genuflecting better than the first-picked altar boys on a Holy Day of Obligation.

Judith C. Owens-Lalude

I was taunted and teased as my classmates passed me. Their verbal *daggers* pierced my inner well-being. I flailed my arms to scoop the papers and notebooks back into my bookbag. I didn't want to lift my head again. I just wanted to camp beneath the brim of my baseball cap, but I couldn't stay in that prayer mode forever–my knee bone pained me. My armpits were soggy and sweat dripped from the tip of my nose and off its columella.

When I reached for the last of my papers, the narrow toe of Mariah's shoe slipped into my peripheral vision. It pointed directly at me. A convulsion erupted inside my clothes. Reluctantly, I shoved my eyeballs upward as my limbs involuntarily floundered about. Mariah stood, looking down at me. I dropped the papers that I held as my eyes scanned the full length of her body, from her pointed-toe shoes to the three-inch part in her hair. *Boy! Oh boy! She's pretty and basketball tall. I love every inch of her height.*

My jaw hinges loosened as I coughed and grunted to clear my throat. With my head tilted backward, as far as it would go, I mumbled, "Maybe, if you're . . ."

The school bell rang. She was gone again. I was still in the supplicant posture. Only now, my knee felt numb.

I snatched the rest of my papers and satchel off the floor. With my *steal* tucked underneath my arm, I bolted down the hallway, turned the corner, and hung in mid-air for some time. When my feet touched the floor, the outer soles of my shoes failed me. Flat on my belly, I watched my satchel glide to the far wall. Fast as a hiccup, I crossed the floor on my knees and seized it. Back on my feet, with my eyes closed, I shook myself Cassius Clay style to ensure nothing was broken. With my bag secured, once again, I was on my way; grateful the hallways were empty, except for Mr. Belkin, who pushed a four-foot-wide, oblong, rag mop down the hall. When he looked my way, I nodded at him with the smile of a new acquaintance and surfed into Mr. Drew's classroom on the rims of my *big dogs*.

"Late again, Mr. Womack?"

Mr. Drew pressed a Physics book, that he had

been reading from, against the buttons of his stark white lab coat. He peered over the half-moon glasses resting on his nose and waited for my reply.

"Yes, sir."

I glided over to my assigned station, glad it was upfront and close to the door. While I waited for Mr. Drew's attack, I searched in my satchel for today's assignments. As I fished through the mix of distorted papers, I prayed to St. Jude to make me like the *Invisible Man* in Ralph Ellison's novel.

"Mr. Womack, could I please have your lab reports?"

Mr. Drew's gruff voice jolted my inner organs. He's gotta be kidding. Tremors moved down my arms to my fingertips. I couldn't hold onto the papers in my hands or the ones crammed inside my bag.

"Got a problem, Mr. Womack?"

"No, sir."

There was a severe tightening of my jaw joints that hung loose seconds ago.

"I need time to organize my stuff."

"Take all that you need. See me after school.

DUNKER

We'll discuss your tardiness and lack of homework."

Mr. Drew closed his physics book with a slam and opened his *Teacher's Grade Book*.

"I'm recording a negative 25 points for your grade today. If you have this problem again, it will lower your grade to a negative 75. Pretty soon, you won't need to show up for class."

Mr. Drew finished the lesson and dismissed the class. An odd kind of peace encased me. That is, until I tried to get up and realized Mr. Drew's heavy hand rested on my rotator cup. I was affixed to my seat. The earth fell away from my feet. Steam radiated from underneath my shirt. Sweat beads dampened my entire body. I was the chocolate heart on the hood of Big Blue, nailed down and melting.

When Mr. Drew released me, I parted my feet and shifted my weight. I peered at the floor where chemical stains had created strange patterns. A dog with pointy ears, balloons on crooked strings, and the two fish blowing bubbles made me stare harder. My cheeks pulled back into a smug smile at the sight of the almost-kissing lips at the arc of my right foot.

Maybe they belonged to Mariah and me.

"Mr. Womack."

My head jolted, just as it did whenever Coach Ben said, Dunker, get out there or Mariah called my name.

"You gawked out of the door during most of the class period, today." Mr. Drew gestured his bald head in that direction. "Indeed, there is physics in the hallway, but what you need is in here. You've got to bring your focus back into this classroom. *Bone-up.* You're about to fail physics." Mr. Drew crossed his arms. "It's happened to some of our top ballplayers. You're excused. Come back after school. Hurry on. Don't be late for lunch." His rubber-tipped wooden pointer indicated the way out.

I went straight to the food queue doing a few goosenecks. Mariah was leaning against the wall waiting to enter the food-service area. Her lipstick was the color of my blood. Her hair flipped at the ends just right and brushed her shoulders each time she moved her head. She was a portrait in motion.

The food service line moved forward. I

zigzagged through the crowd to put myself next to Sly, who was standing behind Mariah. Why did he have to be in this line, at this time? I extended my rebound arm to reach between them for a tray.

"Hey, man. What'cha doin'? You can't be cuttin' line. Step back!"

Sly's grin was too big to be appreciated. I came back at him with an eye that sliced him as if he had blocked my grandstand jump shot. I snatched a tray from the stack. There wasn't room to place it on the rail behind Mariah's. There wasn't even room for me.

With my lips pulled snug, I conjured up my baddest don't-get-in-my-way persona. Sly broadened his grin. He tucked his tray underneath his armpit and sucked in his gut giving me the space I needed to ease between them.

"Hey! Hey! Take it easy, man. You're okay with me," Sly said.

I stood boyfriend-girlfriend close to Mariah. I didn't know if she knew I was there. I inhaled the fragrance of her hair and kissed the back of her neck.

Judith C. Owens-Lalude

Well, if I'd wanted to, I could have, but I didn't want to chance getting slapped silly in the cafeteria. Eyes were already on us. We were both tall and we both played ball. Except, Mariah was baby-doll gorgeous.

She glanced over her shoulder to check out the commotion behind her. "Hey, Dunker," she said and continued pushing her tray along.

"What's up with you today?" I asked.

Mariah nudged her tray along the rails. Her lips moved, but I didn't hear what she said.

She lifted a carton of chocolate milk out of the refrigerated chest and placed it in the upper right corner of her tray. A bowl of gelatin salad was adjusted on the left side of her tray and a golden apple from the fruit basket was placed at 12 o'clock. From underneath the sneeze guard, she chose a roast beef sandwich and positioned it in the center of her tray. Next she pulled a dish of potato rounds and green beans from the steam table down to her tray. They ended up at three o'clock and nine o'clock. I chose the same: milk, salad, apple, sandwich, potato rounds, and green beans. I was her copycat character spinning out of control.

Mariah placed her lunch money next to Miss Charlet's cash register. I did the same. Except, I had a dollar bill and it floated down to the floor. I retrieved it, nearly butting Mariah in the rear with my head. I straightened up and got my change. Carefully following her through the lunchroom, I managed the space between us. I kept an eye on my toes that jutted from beneath the tray, controlling my 12 ½ C's to not clip her heels. My clear-seeing eye checked Mariah's moves. I didn't want her to disappear like she had done numerous times before.

"How's your game?" I asked her.

"Okay. How's your awesome dunk? I haven't seen you working out at the park lately. And you're late for lunch? Where've you been?"

The eye contact with Mariah sent a transverse wave oscillating around my midriff.

"Just got out of class. Mr. Drew held me back. Said he wanted to discuss a few matters with me."

Although Mariah was quiet and didn't turn

to look me in the face, I felt this was my chance.

"Mariah . . ."

"You in trouble, Dunker?"

"Nope! Let's pick a table and sit. We need to talk."

Mariah didn't seem to hear me, and I felt as if my tray was about to flip from my grip. A cafeteria catastrophe was coming after me. I stopped placed my tray on the nearest table.

"Hold up, Mariah. Let's sit here."

"Sure," she said.

Mariah spun around the same as she did for her layup shots. She placed her tray edge head-to-head with mine and slid into the seat in front of me without difficulty. I was cautious when I took my place at the table. Once situated, I pushed my legs out to straddle hers, pulled my feet underneath me, and squirmed to ease the tension in my back. It's always a challenge for two tall people to posture vis-à-vis.

Sitting seemed to be the problem of the day for me. First, it was Mr. Drew's lab stools and now it's these cafeteria contraptions they want us to perch on to eat lunch. Pretty soon I'll be standing year-round. If it's next to Mariah, that's okay.

I propped my wrist against the edge of the table and bowed my head as if I were about to pray. I seemed to be doing that a great deal lately, too. This time, it wasn't for the food that I was about to eat. Instead, it was for Mariah's uninterrupted attention.

I picked up my fork and built a lean-to with my green beans while organizing the words in my head needed for the big question. I was ready to fire it off, but I didn't. There was no need to rush. The cafeteria clock had twenty minutes of lunchtime still on it.

I clamped my teeth onto my roast beef sandwich, yanked out a plug, and started chewing. The meat and bread clung to my palate and hung on. It was choking me to death in Mariah's presence. I grunted to dislodge the half-chewed food.

"Oops!"

"You okay, Dunker?" Mariah asked with a lover's concern.

I nodded that I was. Opening the chocolate

milk carton, I shoved a straw in it and sucked out most of the drink. It softened the wad of food stuck in my mouth. Dislodged, it slid down my throat. All I needed to do, now, was pop the question, not gag to death on a lump of gummy food.

"Mariah . . . a . . . a . . . a."

Her kneecap kissed mine. My leg muscles twitched, my knees locked, and my lean-to collapsed. She moved again. This time, I shifted my weight.

"Hum!" I moaned.

I lifted my eyelids just enough to spy on Mariah eating her lunch and not seeming to notice the contact. By the time I started chewing again, she had only three pieces of potatoes and a lone green bean much too limp to be consumed by a queen.

"Dunker, you okay?"

"Sure. Why you ask?"

"You keep scrunching up your face. Do your feet hurt or something?"

"I'm okay. I was just wondering if we could . . . ah, could . . . ah." I coughed, firing off a nip of roast beef that pierced Mariah's eyebrow. "Sorry," I said, wanting to say more, but couldn't.

Mariah flicked the meat off and continued eating. I tried to speak again, but the words kinked up in my throat with the food I was trying to consume. I couldn't force the words out. With my chin braced on the back of my hand, I mimicked August Rodin's *The Thinker*. Today, I was the duplicate statue going nowhere.

I fashioned the uneaten potato rounds on my plate into a locomotive. I wanted to get aboard it to be taken to the land of cowards. Mariah finished her food and was standing to leave. She held her tray above my head. I ducked and raised my arm to protect my shooting eye.

"You sure you're all right, Dunker?"

"Yeah." I lowered my arm. "A bug was coming at me."

I swatted the air around my head to convince her that there might have been a pesky fly fluttering near my ear. Now, I wanted her to leave. No, I wanted her to stay. No, go. No, stay. I really did want her to stay, at least long enough for me to pop the question.

Judith C. Owens-Lalude

"See you later, Dunker."

Mariah smiled and walked out of my dream-to-be. There has got to be a better way to accomplish this mission. Why couldn't she finish my sentences? Darryl and Darnell always did for each another.

I placed my tray in the dishwashing room's window and headed to class. Mr. Belkin closed the cafeteria door behind me. Although I didn't get to pop the question with Mariah, I told myself not to accept the title of failure and continue to pursue her.

"You can do it," my voice muttered as I continued to convince myself to stay focused. I was now my own cheerleader.

2

Pass the Ball
Dunker

At three o'clock, the final bell rang. School was out. I needed to meet up with Mariah, but Mr. Drew had demanded my presence for an untimely conference. I headed to the Physics Lab. He was standing at the end of the hall, just outside the classroom. As I closed in on him, an *I-gotcha* surfaced on his face that smacked at my academic well-being.

"How you doin', Mr. Drew?"

My voice did a crescendo on mister and mellowed out on Drew. I wanted to sound cool, but I couldn't. I was a stray molecule trapped inside of a mucus membrane with no way out.

"Glad to see you, Mr. Womack. Come on in. We need to talk, son."

Mumbling, Dunker says, "Why me?"

"Say something, Mr. Womack?"

"No, sir!"

Mr. Drew rocked back on his heels until his toes came up off the floor. When he returned to his flat-footedness, he pushed his lab coat back, thrust his hands into his pant pockets, and expanded his chest. He peered over his reading glasses anchored halfway down the broad bridge of his nose. His posture cast a daunting shadow across the floor between my flight path and me.

"Make yourself comfortable, Mr. Womack."

My seat was upfront and close to the exit door. My escape, if necessary, would be foolproof. I cautiously approached it–a small, gray metal disc not much larger than my baseball cap. I'm sure the person in the supply office ordered the smallest stools possible from the purchase catalog. They wanted to get me as did Mr. Drew. With maximum control of my rear end, I lowered it to meet the stool and not land on the floor. I've had enough floor wax in my face to last a decade.

When I sat down, a tingling sensation traveled the length of my spine. It met up with the nerves that spindled down my legs, hitchhiking toward my curled-up toes.

I plopped my bag on the lab bench, fixed the straps to point toward me, and dragged it close. I layered my arms over the top of it. Resting my chin on my bony forearms, I figured that if things got rough, I'd slip my arm through the straps and be out the door with a single kangaroo leap.

"Mr. Womack."

The expression on Mr. Drew's face indicated that I had failed Physics or was close to doing so. I couldn't release the hold I had on my tightened-up toes, so I sucked science-lab air through my nostrils and waited for the verdict.

"Mr. Womack," he called again.

My eyes popped. He had my full attention.

"You were daydreaming in my class today and turned your work in late. Your GPA in this class has fallen drastically. You are about to "foul out" of Physics. Do you want to continue to play ball? Is college still in your plans for the fall?"

Could he be serious? My heart flipped, flopped, and flipped again. My eyeballs dried up. I couldn't blink. I couldn't even take in enough air to clearly note what was happening to me. I nodded my head to indicate an *I do*. I was having a heart attack, right here in the Physics Lab sitting on an undersized stool. Who'd believe that Raymond James "Dunker" Womack, one of the greatest basketball shooting guards ever, departed this earth in such an undignified manner?

"If you do?" I braced myself. Mr. Drew tilted forward. He was coming at me again, "You'll have to be more focused on your work."

"I can do that, sir."

Mr. Drew braced his weight on the tabletop podium at the end of the lab bench. He aimed his body toward me. Shifting arm-to-arm, he shot a look at me that penetrated my basketball soul. Mr. Drew was a baking soda rocket ready for takeoff. He stiffened his back and adjusted his weight again.

DUNKER

"If you've got a problem, come see me. We'll talk about it."

"Yes, sir."

This time Mr. Drew took the stance of a coach with his eye on the play but didn't stop focusing on me. He dipped his right shoulder. He kept giving me attention that I didn't want. The daggers he released from his eyes, came straight to mine. They made my pupils bleed.

"Is there something I can help you with, Mr. Womack?"

His voice chilled my eardrums.

"No, sir."

My words punctuated the space between us. He can't help me, not with this problem.

Mr. Drew studied me but didn't dismiss me. He lifted his upper body off the podium and pushed his lab coat to the rear again. He had a way of doing that, that made me uneasy. This time he closed his eyes. He turned coins and keys over in his pockets. I thought he was going to take a hiatus, but his eyes reopened with a more intensified gaze.

"Got a question?" Mr. Drew asked.

He thrust his right ear toward me.

"No, sir!" I said as I would to a recruiting sergeant who yapped a command in my face.

"All right. From now on you'll come to class with your work organized and ready to turn it in. And be punctual, or you'll be here with me next year. That'll give us time to put things in their proper perspectives."

"Yes, sir," I said in my strongest voice to let Mr. Drew know that I took him seriously.

He scared me bad. I kept thinking, no ball, no scholarship, no life. I'd be a dead man trying to play ball.

"Goodbye, Mr. Womack. Be sure to complete your experiment on magnesium tomorrow. Don't let the clock run out on you."

"Y-ye. Yes, sir!"

When my nerves reconnected, I pulled my satchel to my lap. I bounced my bookbag, soothing it as if it were a baby. Mr. Drew returned to his station to start a blackboard configuration. I studied the back of his head, not sure what to do.

DUNKER

Loud, exciting voices from the hall cut through the tic-tack of the chalk tapping against the blackboard. I crooked my neck and glanced at the door. No one was there. The voices that pricked my hearing had moved on.

"Good day, Mr. Womack," Mr. Drew said. He didn't even turn to see if I was leaving.

"I'm gone, sir. I'm out of here."

I moved as if firecrackers were lit beneath my stool. I rushed out of the door, through the halls, passing at least a hundred and twenty lockers before I fell against one. I shook my head in disbelief. It rattled me to think that Mr. Drew might mess with my basketball career and scholarships. He could flat-out fail me, which would blow my chances for everything I wanted right now. I'd be left with no All-Star team, no college, no prom, and no Mariah. Not to mention my life with Mom, Dad, and Grandma which would spiral into a hellish turmoil. I've got to get Mr. Drew off my case and put my life back on track.

When I took geometry in the ninth grade, I had top scores. The equation for my life was intact, thanks to Pythagorean's Theorem, ($a^2 + b^2 = c^2$). That's *basketball² + grades² = college²*. This year, Mariah caused a mathematical dilemma. I had to cancel Pythagorean's Theorem and replace it with the Womack Theorem: $a^2 + b^2 + c^2 = d^2$ (*basketball² + grades² + Maria² = college²)*. If one of the values changed to a negative, there will be no All-Star basketball, prom, or college. There goes my arms around Mariah and the kisses with them. I'm in hot shit.

I hurried to the gym and entered the Boys' Locker Room. The stench of over-used sneakers, the musty socks, along with the sweaty bodies, fought in my nostrils. At my locker, I fumbled with the lock until it sprang open. I dressed in my practice jersey and wasted no time, joining my teammates for a bounce-and-pass drill. I hoped that Coach Ben wouldn't notice me, but he did and blew his whistle that signaled for me to drop out of line.

"You're late, Dunker. Give me sixty and a ten."

Why was Coach Ben riding my back? It

wasn't like I was out messing around or doing something wrong. It was Mr. Drew who kept me parked on that undersized stool for too long.

I separated from the team and did as Coach said. On my belly, I tucked my toes underneath me, and pushed my weight up and down, pumping my arms as fast as Big Blue's pistons. Beads of perspiration surfaced on my 'ceps; sweat covered my entire back; my forehead was drippy. When the calisthenics was done, I started the ten laps around the gym.

Sly and the Bender twins pointed and jeered each time I passed them, causing me to miss my timing and stumble. As I recovered, Sly fake-passed the ball to me. I misstepped again. That gave them a chuckle, at my expense. Their athletic teeth sank deep into my basketball hide–that hurt. I finished my laps bent over and heaving.

Sly squatted to get in my face. "Hey, man. Talk to ya girl yet?" he asked with a silly grin on his face. "Cat got your tongue? Or, has Mama putcha in the doghouse?"

Judith C. Owens-Lalude

The screech of his voice rippled my skin. I had the mind to reach up and grab his throat with both hands and ring it dish-rag style. Instead, I straightened up to prepare for the next drill. Coach Ben blew his whistle to change the routine.

"Dribble, drive, and pass the ball to the next man. No hesitations. No misses," he said.

When the ball came to me, I slapped it, took it downcourt, and passed it to Sly with a centrifugal thrust powerful enough to carve a sphere in the center of his gut. It didn't. He grunted as he caught the ball and dropped out of line. Only the captain could do that. He dribbled the full length of the court, made a layup shot, rebounded it, brought the ball back upcourt and initiated a double-line drill. Nice! But I wanted to put that chicken head on his ass.

Sly bounce-passed the ball to me. I snapped it up and shoved it back to him with a bucking kick. He sent it back to me with equal force.

"Take it on downcourt!" he shouted.

I did. I laid it up and caught my own rebound. Dribbling back upcourt, I fancied the ball between my legs before passing it to Jake. He took the *pill*, laid it up, and dribbled back to the lineup. He passed the ball to Darryl. Darryl completed the drill and sent the ball to Darnell. He did the same and passed the ball to me. Instead of taking the pill back downcourt, I dribbled in place, cool-rocked my hips, and flaunted my stuff.

That's when *I drifted off with Mariah* and mistakenly passed the ball to one of the Bender twins instead of Jake. When the ball came back, I never saw it. That move put me flat on my back with Coach Ben packing ice on the left side of my face. It chilled my eye while the humiliation fried the rest of me.

"I think you got yourself a shiner, Dunker. You know the rules about getting hurt on the court. Get dressed. Go on home and put ice on your face. We probably won't be seeing you tomorrow. I'll send an incident report to the nurse's office and give your parents a call."

With their forearms braced underneath my armpits, the twins said, "Let's go."

I was lifted as if I were a feathered-filled sack. I've got to put this situation with Mariah behind me. If

Judith C. Owens-Lalude

I'm absent from practices more than three times, I won't be allowed to tryout for the All-Star team. At this rate, I am headed to no ball game, no graduation, no girl, no kiss, no college, and now, an eye that might not be seeing what it needs to see.

3

Big Blue and a Black Eye
Dunker

From underneath a full sun, I stood next to Big Blue, top dropped, and parked nose-close to the school wall. I couldn't squeeze between them if I wanted to. I wasn't thinking when I pulled into the parking slot. Normally, I don't get that close to anything. Plus, I wanted to put a football field between Blue and the rods on each side of him. The guys at school never cared if they banged Blue with their car doors. Yet, the smallest ping or nick pained me. I broke gallons of sweat to keep him looking as if he had just rolled off the assembly line when he was showcased at the 1939 World's Fair in New York. Dad informed me it wasn't long after that, that Grandaddy got Blue as a gift from the Ford family.

Shifting my thoughts and ready to go home, I threw my bookbag on the passenger's seat and watched it plummet to the floor. I drew my leg up, ready to hurdle myself over the driver's door. The bruised eye blocked my move. I opened the door instead and eased in behind the steering wheel. I bounced on the seat and tugged at my gym shorts stuck to my butt 'til I could sit on the scorching split bench. So much for a drop-top.

After fiddling with the gearshift to get Blue into neutral, I turned the ignition switch on and pulled the choke button. The engine turned over. When Big Blue purred, I pushed the choke back in, put the gear shift in reverse, slowly backed him out of the parking space, and eased him to the curb.

My foot came up off the clutch when an opening appeared in the traffic. I revved the motor and merged Blue into the flow of cars. I didn't know where people were going, but I was headed home. I turned my head to allow my right eye to monitor the traffic. I didn't want Big Blue to collide with a moving target. If he did, Dad'd stomp out my driving privileges, Mom would yammer in my ear, and Toby'd mock me while

DUNKER

Grandma got in my face to shake her rosary and recite the prayer she created for such occasions:

> Holly Mary Mother of God; Saint Michael, the Archangel; and all the guardian angels above, look down on my big boy–the little one, too. Protect them against all the evils of the world. If by chance, a hooligan raises a mean hand against one of them, I humbly ask that you cast him into the fires of hell without a hamburger or cold drink. And don't allow him to take his jalopy with him. I pray this in the name of the Almighty, as I beg you, too, to keep my boys in your grip.

I turned onto Plato Street, a narrow road leading to our driveway. The houses lining the street were all the same, red-brick two stories with double picture windows, mailboxes to the right of the door, and four steps stretched across the fronts that lead up to scarlet-painted porches. Most of which had heavy green and white metal chairs, gliders, or rockers on them. Several had wooden porch swings at the far side that

Judith C. Owens-Lalude

hung on chains dangling from the ceiling.

Coming up to 2117, my house, I pushed in on the clutch and pressed the brake paddle. Glad to be home, I easy-rolled Blue over the gutter at the foot of the driveway and parked behind Dad's pickup truck.

I sighed out loud and turned the key to off. When I tried to block the thought of going into the house, the sun that smacked the back of my neck caused my eye to swell shut and just about pop out of my head. I sat. I thought for a moment about basketball, heat, pain, school, and Oh Yes! Mariah. I dragged my foot back toward the seat preparing to spring into motion.

Once again, the mega pain from my eye forced me back down. I opened the door. Swing my legs out, I stood up without incident, but my first step clobbered Mama's irises and her daffodils that I suggested, a hundred times for her to be plant them on the east side of the driveway. "Can't. Won't be able to see them from the kitchen window. And they won't get enough sun over there," she'd say.

Too exhausted to struggle with the weight of my satchel, I banged the car door shut and left it behind. Toby can get it later. He needed the exercise to pump up the muscles in his puny arms. Whenever he flexed them, I'd get the magnifying glass to see the minuscule humps he said were there. Who knows, he might get a girl cute as Mariah and lock his skinny limbs around her waist.

"Hehehe! Ouch!"

I reclaimed my balance, cupping my swollen eye to keep it still, I moved toward the house. But I didn't go inside before I knocked the toes of my shoes against the step. Mom didn't appreciate dirt on her *Grandma-clean* floor. I squeezed the handle of the screen door. I didn't budge for what seemed like a long stretch of minutes. Meticulously, I eased the door toward me and stepped inside the kitchen, fearing the sound of Mom's voice when she saw me and my muddy feet.

"My God! What happened to you? Take those shoes off. Sit down."

Mom's words flipped out as she brushed her wet hands up and down the front of her apron, leaving an uneven track of dark blue blotches. My feet were anchored in place. It was Mom who aimed my body to face the kitchen chair and gave me a gentle love shove to ease the tension.

"Go ahead. Sit down. Coach Ben called. He said you might need an extra day off from practice for your eye. Now I see why."

I ambled toward a chair angled and ready to receive me. I'd never noticed it before, but today the sight of its sufficient bottom made me smile. I collapsed on it with confidence and assurance. My weight fell against the kitchen table. I leaned on my left elbow to keep my body from sliding out of the chair. I hadn't realized how fatigued I was until I heard Mom speak. I was glad she was home. Paco, my dog, smelled the cereal in my pant pocket and jumped up and down, pawing my leg. Too weak to lift him, I brushed his wet nose aside. Dad circled me from my blind side to my seeing side. "Boy! What were you thinking about that took your mind off of what you were doing and got you that shiner?"

"Don't know," was all I could think to say.

"Of all the days for you to be home," I muttered.

"What did you say, son?"

"Nothing, Dad."

When I saw Dad's truck in the driveway, I hoped that he had left it there while he visited Toby's school. Toby hated for Dad to drive the truck over there. It backfired, scaring the kids so bad the little ones wet their pants.

"Wash up, son. Get something to eat. Go rest," Dad said and reached for the newspaper just in time to see Mom coming at me with a beefy-red steak.

"Hey! What'cha doin' with that good cut of beef?" Dad moved in close. He cocked his head for a better look. "I just bought that steak."

With a severe sharpness in her voice, Mom said, "Taking care of your son's eye."

She laid the half-frozen slab across my face. I flinched when the icy crystals touched down on my searing eye. The pain that registered off of the chart, forced tears out of my good eye.

"That'll control the swelling, dear."

While Mom's words cradled my ears, Dad's lips quivered. "That's an expensive cut of steak!" He said again, to make his point.

"And I'm putting it to good use."

Mom cut a mean look at Dad as she shifted her hips and turned her back to him. She continued to doctor my eye and pretended Dad wasn't there.

Grandma's house slippers shuffled across the floor above my head. Next, they plopped down the

Judith C. Owens-Lalude

stairs.

Grandma gasped as she came off the last step. With her rosary clamped down on her heart, she rushed me. With her head lowered in prayer, she struck her chest three times.

"Holy Mary Mother of God what has happened to my grandson."

Mom anchored her hands around the meat, raised her elbows, like a kite taking flight, and shifted the steak with all the exaggeration she could muster up. She pivoted her hips to let Dad know who was in charge of the meat. With a grunt, he smacked the newspaper against his leg. My back arced as if I were popped with an oversized rubber band.

Smiling, Mom warned, "Keep still."

I wanted to reach out to hug her, but my arms wouldn't move. If she were Mariah, they'd coil around her mocking a cartoon snake looping around a tree limb.

"What are you staring at, son?" Mom asked. Embarrassed, I closed my good eye.

"Just thinking, Mom."

I didn't need to open my eyes to know Grandma was back in my space. Her jasmine sachet alterted me when she poked my shoulder as if to arouse a drunk.

"You okay, Dunker?"

"Yeah, Grandma. I'm doing fine just got hurt."

"You sure, boy? Cause, if it was one of them ruffians who put his fist to your eye, I'll choke him with this rosary sure as I'm clasping it. And, he'll never see those pearly gates of heaven. He'll be lucky if he gets into purgatory. I promise you that."

The chime of the crystal beads above my head made me open my good eye. Grandma was shaking her fisted rosary at the heavens above her head.

"Daughter?" She said and searched Mom's face for an answer.

"It's okay, Mother. Dunker got hurt at basketball practice. He'll be fine."

Mom planted a reassuring kiss on the top of grandma's bent-in-prayer head. That's when Paco heard the newspaper crunch. The bottoms of his ears bulged. Squatted close to Dad's chair, he reared back on his hind legs. Without an invitation, he leaped into Dad's lap and nested underneath the newspaper. Together, they waited for the school bus.

"Move over, boy. Give me some room."

Judith C. Owens-Lalude

Mom and I laughed out loud.

"Ouch!" I moaned.

I didn't want so much fuss over my eye. I just wanted a little doctoring. Now, I needed to escape to mull over my thoughts and prioritize them.

"Please, Mom. Can you hurry and finish with my eye? I need to split."

Paco, postured at the front door, barked at the hissing sound of the hydraulic brakes that announced his young master's arrival. Toby vaulted off the last step of the school bus. Swinging his satchel in one hand and his lunchpail in the other, he raced along the walkway and up the front steps. He burst through the front door, hollering, "I'm home! Where's Mom?"

"In the kitchen with your brother," Dad said.

Hearing Toby's question, Dunker said, "What's it to ya?"

"Cause I wanna know."

"Mom's cooking steak on my eye. Why don't you get lost? Better yet, get my bookbag out of the car."

Toby scrunched his face and glanced cocked-eyed at Mom, who said with an uncompromising but cushy voice, "Get your brother's bag, dear."

DUNKER

Toby dropped his school satchel close to my foot, where I'd trip and break my neck if I got up. I jabbed my fist up toward his nose.

"Get that bag out of my way."

Toby turned himself over and farted a big stink. I tried to kick his butt, but Mom's steak and the pain blocked my move. Toby stomped across the floor and shoved open the screen door. Strong-footed, he bounded down the steps letting Mom know he didn't want to serve me.

Out of my good eye, on the kitchen door side of me, I watched Toby hook his fingers into the corners of his mouth. He stretched his lips as he glared into Big Blue's side-view mirror, dangling his tongue so close to the glass he could have tasted it. I'd shave the tip of it off, if it wouldn't bleed on Blue. Now he's poking his fingers at the mirror. Toby knows he's turning the knife he jammed into my back. The boy's making my skin crawl. I'm gonna dice and fry his behind to a crisp . . . soon as Mom lets me out from under this steak. Toby finished his clowning and went around to the passenger's side of Big Blue and opened the door. I knew he caught hold of the bookbag straps, pulled on it and nothing happened. Leaning further into the car, he'd tug it again. I knew it sprang up off the footboard, wrestled him to the ground. Squirmed from beneath it, he was finally squatted alongside the bloated bundle.

"One, two, three," Toby grunted and straightened his legs. "You long tall beanpole. You should'a sent a weightlifter to get this."

Toby lugged the load into the house and dropped it just inside the kitchen door. A rush of vibrating waves rippled beneath my feet.

Mom lifted the meat off my face. She patted my shoulder in a way that let me know she cared about my agony.

"Eat and go rest your eye like Dad said."

"Free at last," I sang, stretching my legs.

I wanted to shake my head to get the kinks out of my neck, but I thought about my eye and rotated my shoulders instead.

After I washed my hands, I ingested Mom's fried chicken, mashed potatoes with gravy, and collard greens, not stopping to breathe or glanced up from my plate.

"I'm out of here, Mom."

DUNKER

Glad to end this day, I kissed her on the cheek and escaped to the solitude of my room. Without bending over, I squatted to unlace my gym shoes. I toed them and the socks off. Afterward, I removed my shorts and shirt and dropped them in the pile with a cluster of mismatched gym shoes, books, and cloth mingled in rumpled beddings. I nudged the heap with my barefoot, 'til it was all beneath the bed.

I gripped a few bits of the cereal loops scattered on the floor with my toes. A swift upward movement landed them in Tipper's cage. He hopped off his hamster wheel to cram the loops into his mouth. Satisfied, he wiggled his whiskers as he scurried to the back corner of his cage where he bore underneath the shredded newspaper. From his bulging cheeks, he regurgitated the cereal. The well he created filled quickly with it. Tipper never noticed that I stared at him out of my good eye while I waited for an indication of some kind of thank-you. None came.

I stretched out on my bed to let the coolness of the pillows beneath my head sooth the back of my neck. I dragged a stray one across my chest and squeezed it. Coach Ben's mantra played in my head. "If you want to be successful on the court, you gotta think about moving with the ball."

Yeah! That's it. I'll rush up to Mariah and stand close to her, saying what I gotta say with soft words. She'll slap my lips off the front of my face. It'd be better to write a note and slip it to her, but she'd squish it and trash it. I could scroll a message across the chalkboard in her homeroom. She'd see it first thing in the morning and everyone else would, too. I'd be the joke of the day. I'll bite the bullet, stand face-to-face with her and pop the question that I've repeated a thousand times in my mind without stuttering once.

I released the pillow and got out of bed. I cocked my head to check out my eye in the dresser mirror. It was an ugly, blue-black swollen-shut orb. I slanted my back, dropped my right shoulder, dangled my right arm, and shifted my jaw. A dude looked back at me. Even though the top of his head was cut off when I straightened my body, the dude in the mirror was still cool. I put my words in playbook order, leaned toward the image again, and let them go.

"Mariah, can I take you to . . . ?"

"Whatcha say, Dunker? You wanna take who? Where?" Toby mocked.

DUNKER

Snatched out of my attitude, I yelled, "Get your butt out of here, or I will . . ."

I snatched up one of my 12 ½ C's and hurled it at his head. It clipped the doorframe and dropped on its side. At first, I didn't see Paco on the heels of Toby. I can't understand why he wants to hang out with him, but only a dog would.

"Who you gonna take where?"

Toby was back and ticking me off. With one clean sweep of my forearm, I moved everything from under my bed to one side. I caught hold to the mate of my sneaker and flung it. The sock inside of it landed on Tipper's cage and, again, the shoe hit the door frame. Toby grabbed his head.

"I'm gonna tell Mom on you. You big, fat, stinky-footed, half-baked, fool."

I slammed the door and wished I had done to Toby what he was trying to convince Mom that I had. Thereupon, she could put Daddy's steak on his head and shove him and the meat into the refrigerator 'til his prom day.

The pressure from my anger throbbed behind my eyeball where I didn't need it. I snatched an empty pop bottle from the dresser. Stretched out on the bed, I cooled my bruise with the bottom of it. That conjured up memories of Dad's meat on my eye. I shivered with laughter. When I quieted down, I heard Tipper on his wheel. The repetitive motion eased me into a light sleep.

The next morning, I was up earlier than usual to work on my school assignments. In the bathroom, I stood in front of the medicine cabinet mirror. I held down the eyelid of my good eye and peeped through the slit of the puffy, purple-blue one–not as swollen as yesterday. I flushed my face with cool water but didn't let soap near my eye. I lathered the rest of me in the shower.

Ready to get dressed, I noticed my shoes weren't in their usual place, side-by-side at the foot of it. Instead, one leaned against the doorframe while its mate lay dead in the hall. In the center of the floor was a sock without a mate. I shoved my left dog into it. When I was about to lower my head to find its partner, I caught a view of it on top of Tipper's cage. I snatched it off and pulled it over my foot. All five digits on my left foot went through the open toe of it. At a glimpse, my good eye noted a brown fur ball

DUNKER

buried beneath the matching colors of my socks.

"You! You little pint-sized beast! You chewed up my sock. Won't be no cereal for you today. I suggest you dine on your stash." I thumped the cage to let Tipper know that I meant business. He ignored me.

"And back at you," I snorted.

I rolled off the socks and got a fresh pair from the drawer. After finishing my homework, I packed my bookbag. On my way out of the room, I *X'ed* another May day on the wall calendar. The June one was coming at me fast.

Going down the stairs, but not rushing, I inhaled the aroma of breakfast. Mom's kitchen was the place to be in the early morning hours. Today, I devoured several slices of bacon and wolfed down eggs. While gulping a jelly jar full of milk, I stole Toby's bread off his plate. Afterward, I grabbed my bag and rushed out the backdoor. His chin grazed his chest. I couldn't resist the toast. It was heaped with apple butter just the way I like it.

"You gonna be sorry, you knotty-legged giraffe. Eat my toast and die!"

Judith C. Owens-Lalude

I tossed my bookbag on the passenger seat. Still seething, I blew my breath on Big Blue's side-view mirror. With my shirttail, I rubbed Toby's fingerprints off of it and swallowed the last of his toast.

Settled on the driver's seat, I put Blue in gear and took off. I didn't bother to warm him up. I wanted to get to school before Mariah. No red lights stopped me. Timing was on my side. I stood in the school bus drop-off area, goose-necking when I didn't have to. I could see over the top of most heads.

"They're here!" I said.

The buses pulled into their designated posts. When the doors popped open, the schoolyard swarmed with a Tsunami of students, blocking me on all four sides. Not one face that I saw belonged to Mariah until . . .

"There she is!" I waved frantically. "Hey, Mariah, hold up." I shouted. She didn't hear me. I pushed forward, waving and shouting more. "Hey! Hey! Mariah." No answer. I gathered all the wind I had and let it rip, "Maaariiiahhh!"

DUNKER

She turned, looking in my direction, as did most of the folks on the schoolyard and those still getting off the buses. Mariah flashed a perfect smile, waved, and moved in with the girlfriends. I was petrified until one of my teammates broke the spell.

"Hey! Hey! Wait up," Sly said.

From out of nowhere, he was blocking my pursuit as if we were on opposing teams. He couldn't have picked a worse time to plant himself in front of me. I think he waited around just to tap dance on my nerve endings.

"How's the eye, man? We're all sorry about what happened in practice."

"The eye's okay. Move it, Sly. I don't have time for you."

"Damn, she's gone."

"What did you say?"

I stepped past Sly. Turning my body sideways, I lifted my pack of books above my head and weaved my body through the crowd. Once inside the school building, I was bumped pinball-style, body-to-body until finally, I stood side-by-side with Mariah at her

Judith C. Owens-Lalude

locker. Her sun-warmed body filled my nose with floral fragrances. Boy oh boy, she smelled honeysuckle soap clean and magnolia fresh.

Laid back, I said, "Mariah."

"Dunker. Your eye! What happened?"

"Got hit with the ball in practice yesterday."

"But your eyeball's red."

"That's because I've been up since 4:00 a.m. I had a mound of English homework to do. And, I'm behind in Physics. Mr. Drew's been harassing me. I want to keep playing ball and get a good scholarship."

"Hang in there. I've heard from my top-pick colleges. So far, it's looking good," Mariah said and thumbed my bag back up on my shoulder. Her touch seemed unreal.

"You okay?" she asked.

"I'm fine. But you and me . . . we need to talk."

"Come on, Mariah. We don't want to be late to class," the girlfriends shouted.

"See you, Dunker. Got to go. We'll talk later."

Mariah slammed her locker door closed. She reeled almost knocking me down. She was gone, leaving the clatter of metal doors, up and down the hall, ringing in my ears. I slid my free hand deep into my front, right pant pocket and headed for my first class. My legs moved as if a lumberjack's log was cuffed to each ankle. The tardy bell sounded louder than usual.

Trouble was at my back. Six-feet tall with a black eye, there was no way to sneak into Mrs. Roth's English class. Besides, everyone knows that she has eyes in the back of her head–for some reason, most of teachers seemed to. When I entered the room, she was posting *must-dos* on the blackboard.

Not turning around Mrs. Roth said, "Mr. Womack, you're late. Write a two-page paper. Let me know what delayed you."

She knew I didn't have time for extra work. Disgruntled, I took my seat at the far side of the classroom, next to the wall of windows. I retrieved yesterday's "must-do" list and hurriedly scribbled today's list on the back of it. On the second sheet of paper, I prioritized the assignments, putting the shorter ones at the top and working my way down to the longer ones.

Just as I finished, the sunlight shifted. It bathed my face with a warmth that lured me into a daydream I couldn't resist. I went willingly, but not intentionally.

Mariah reached out for my hand. I was king. She was my queen. We danced and snuggled. I turned her around and dipped her over my arm. Just as I was about to kiss her, the bell rang. When I blinked, she faded into the shrubs.

"Come back! Don't go!" I said with a silent voice.

"Mr. Womack!"

"You weren't with us today. You never opened your English book or took notes."

Mrs. Roth stood over me. Her pointer finger aimed at my notebook.

"Add one more page to your essay. Let me know what you saw out of that window that captivated you so you couldn't concentrate on your work today."

Mrs. Roth tapped her fingernail twice on my desk and walked away.

"Yes, ma'am."

DUNKER

I bit down on my ink pen, knowing I couldn't tell her what I saw. She would never understand. I wasn't sure myself.

4

Dunker Scores
Dunker

The next day, when I was leaving school, I headed down the hall leading to the gym and on out to the student parking lot. Sly was coming from a perpendicular hall on his way to practice. He had a musketeer at each hip. I couldn't for 100,000 free throws understand why the twins wanted to hang with him.

"Hey! Dunker, wait up," Sly called.

He and his two sides created a three-man rush attack on me. I took a stop stance before I stepped to the side and sprinted down the hall.

"Not now, Sly. I gotta move on. Dig you and your sides later," I said, as I passed them without as much as a nod."

DUNKER

I didn't want small talk with a fool right now. I turned the last corner and headed out the door. I bypassed the parking lot, 'cause Big Blue was at home. I didn't have money to gas him up and couldn't ask Dad for it. He wasn't in a tolerant frame of mind this morning. He was still pissed off about his steak on my black eye. Even though he wasn't standing next to me, his voice strummed on my eardrums. "Gotta wait for your allowance, son." Dad forgets that I have business to take care of: Mariah, the prom, flowers, and all that stuff. I needed an advance on my allowance, and a raise also.

The walking was good for me. It gave me time to strategize. I cut through the park on my way home. I knew Mariah would be there. She practices on center court to fine-tune her half-court shots. I hoped Coach Ben understood why I'm not at practice today. He told Mom I might need an extra day for my eye; it's still smarting. I'll work double hard at the next practice to make up for the lost time.

There she is, hooping it up. Damn, Mariah's good. I had to smack my chest. Whenever I saw her, it pounded with a heart-attack beat. If she's handling the *pill*, that beat does a double-time. "Damn! She's good. Enough of this."

My big dogs step-stumbled down the hill, circled the pond, and crossed the park to the basketball court. My feet and legs felt strange, I wasn't sure if I'd still be standing when I got close enough to Mariah to steal the ball from her.

Delilah was at her post on the park bench. She chewed gum and read a girly teen novel that made me want to poke my finger down my throat.

"Hey, little sis. How you doin'?" I said to her as I glanced toward the court to check out Mariah.

"I'm okay."

"What happened to your eye?" Delilah asked as she squinted for a better look.

"Got hit with the ball at practice yesterday," I said, still digging Mariah's moves with my good eye.

"Does it hurt?"

"Not bad," I answered, monitoring Mariah's moves.

"Going to any car shows this summer?"

"Un-huh." Eyes still on Mariah, I slid my cap around backward. "Going to the Street Rod Show in August."

"Where's it going to be?"

"Right here in Louisville. At the fairgrounds. Gonna be hundreds of cars there. There'll be hot rods, street rods, and vintage cars, too."

I wanted to dismiss Delilah. She's okay with me, but I didn't want to share my car-thing with a girl, not even the sister of Mariah.

I put my satchel down on the bench next to Delilah and turned my entire body to face Mariah. She was the reason I came to the park. I parted my feet, put my hands on my hips, sported my come-on-let's-get-it-on persona and waited for the cue.

"Hey, Dunker."

There it was.

"How about some one-on-one?"

"You got it."

I joined Mariah on the turf where she cool-bounced the ball, planted my feet almost a yard from hers, but didn't get too close to her. She never stopped bouncing the ball until she pumped it into a rhythm that set my soul on fire. I had the inclination to fix my lips against hers, but I knew I had to stay focused.

Leaning in, I popped the ball from Mariah's bounce and gave it a hand-to-hand until I established a steady metronome beat. I shot Mariah a macho look with my good eye. She huffed and looked away, causing my flirt to ricochet off her high cheekbone.

"I'm all yours, sweets. Let's get it on."

I crouched low. My heels pulsated against the pavement. I was ready to take her on. Mariah was tough. She played hardball and played with grit. She never eased up on her game just because she was a girl. On a good day, she'd blow me away, but here I am today, taking on the challenge. God help me. I scratched the basketball with my thumbnail, creating a crucifix. I'd done that often in tight games. I slapped the *pill* and passed it to Mariah. She pulled it to her chest, right where I wanted to be, bounced it with one hand, and raised her free one to guard me. I stole the ball, squatted again, and came up for my first jump shot that hit the rim. I rushed in for a Womack

DUNKER

Slam Dunk, but Mariah was already underneath the basket springing up for the rebound, bumping my sore eye on her way up; pain bells harped in my head. She was palming the ball above her head. My arm blocked what I thought was coming next. She dribbled, turned counterclockwise, backed into me, and came straight up off the court. She was an angel in flight.

"Two points," she smirked.

My eye throbbed, her halo slipped, and the angelic wings disappeared. Horns grew from the base of her braids. I shook off the double hurt, stood firm, and caught the ball chest-passed to me.

I scurried to the top of the key. That put the space needed between Mariah and my eye. Now I could score big. I pivoted in circles and passed the ball between my legs. I didn't need both eyes for this dance.

"Come on! Come on! Give it up, Dunker!"

Mariah's hands and arms were everywhere. She was all over me like chicken pox. She had my case covered. I hunkered lower before I took to the air with a hook shot. Just as I did, Mariah heaved; her bust rose and the ball thumped the rectangle. Mariah came from beneath my armpit and tipped the ball in.

"Two points," she hollered loud enough for anybody in the park to hear.

My legs buckled. My body wavered. I missed shot after shot. My eye and my lack of sleep were kicking my butt. I nearly knocked Mariah down more than once. I "T" my hands. "Enough! Timeout. We need to talk."

"Sure, Dunker. What's up? Everything okay?"

"Yeah, yeah. Things are okay."

"Is it your eye?"

Mariah wrinkled her nose to study my face. When she raised her hand, I backed away from her almost touch. Something I thought I'd never do, but the pain was still raw. The thought of being touched drew my gut into a tight twist.

"It's fine."

I bounced the ball trying to maintain some kind of cool. It didn't work, so I anchored it on my left hip and clutched Mariah's upper arm with my right hand, making sure she was on my good-eye side. I made gargantuan steps as I pulled her down the court. She stared at me in disbelief as she doubled-stepped to keep up with my pace. I don't know why I took her there. Maybe, because it was the right place to talk. Underneath the security of the dangling basketball net, I spun Mariah around and blurted, "Mariah! Go to the prom with me."

I didn't miss a word, but when they came out, my bladder filled to its capacity. I was about to wet my pants. I bounced the ball doing a pee-pee dance. This was not gonna happen to me. "Hang with me a bit longer, Lord. I need you and a few of your guiding saints."

"What did you say, Dunker."

"Just talking to myself. Saying a prayer I was sure only the Lord could hear."

Mariah hadn't answered the big question. She was still staring at me. The color in her face had faded from a smooth chestnut brown to a blotchy mud-brown. I could never remember her looking so drawn. Maybe I was too much for her on the court, or she didn't want to go to the Senior Prom with me.

Rejection crept over me worse than a bad rash. I stopped dancing and turned my head to peer over my shoulder. I calculated the distance from my standing point, to the end of the court, back across the park, around the pond, and over the hill. That's when an angelic voice sang, "Dunker, I'd like to go to the prom with you." I must be in heaven, I thought.

Mariah's face was so lit up, I wanted to say *I love you*, but I couldn't. The words were held captive in my throat.

"Wow!" I said instead and started breathing again.

I rotated my head and shoulders to challenge the freaky feelings that invaded me.

"Let's go, Mariah. Mama's waiting for us. We're gonna get in trouble if you don't. Come on. You know what Mama said about being out on the court too late. And I got homework to do."

"Gotta go, Dunker."

Mariah tapped the ball from my hold and skipped off in the direction of Delilah's voice.

DUNKER

"Hey. Wait up. Just tell me. Who invented little brothers and little sisters?"

"Hehehe!" We chuckled and waved goodbye.

I rushed Mariah, stole the ball back, and turned my rear to her. This was my last chance to make an impression. With my thumb firmly on the ball, I was more serious this time when I drew the sign of the cross on it. I heaved and pumped the ball. When I felt in control of myself, I took a stoop stance and gave the *pill* up to the Lord with all the passion I had. The ball arched the full length of the court. When it was over the basket, it dropped in and didn't even nick the rim. It was nothing but net. I followed the ball downcourt, scooped it up, and passed it to Mariah with a wink from my good eye.

"See you tomorrow," I said.

I got my satchel off the bench. I headed home with a boatload of good feelings.

"She likes me. I know she likes me," I chanted to the space around me.

I ran back across the park doing three-foot jump shots and making big hoops I didn't need a ball for. At the backdoor, I clutched the handle of the screen door, for what seemed forever. I eased it open, stepped into Mom's kitchen, and let my satchel drop to the floor.

"Where have you been, Mr. Raymond James Womack?"

The frown lines that crossed Mom's forehead deepened as she spoke. She perched her hands on her hip bones as her chest ballooned from behind the apron bib. You don't keep Mom's dinner waiting. PERIOD. No exceptions.

"Wait! Mom." I raised both hands. "Don't get upset. I had to ask Mariah to go to the prom with me. That took time."

"Well. Come sit down. What did she say?"

Mom held onto her apron tail as she waited for the answer.

"Yes! of course," I said with assurance. "Gotta go to the bathroom, Mom. I'll be right back."

When I returned, Mom's frown lines had disappeared. She was smiling at me and had let go of her apron.

"Let's sit down and eat. Prom day will come

quickly. There's a lot that needs to be done."

Mom glanced at Toby who sat at the kitchen table eavesdropping.

"Your big brother's taking Mariah to the prom," she said to him as if he were invited to be part of the conversation.

Toby got up on his knees. He stretched himself across the table until the smell of fish and coleslaw from his mouth met my nose.

"Dunker, you going to the prom?" he asked.

Toby was over the line, in my space. I palmed his shoulders and shoved him back.

"Sit down. You'll get clued later. Maybe."

Mom stacked my plate with fried fish, coleslaw, and fried green tomatoes. When I finished eating, she gestured her head to let me know that I should get her notepad kept next to the telephone. It was a small pink tablet with midnight-blue lines, curled corners, and coffee-stained pages.

I put my plate in the sink and studied the sudsy water before getting the pad. I wondered if Mariah had really said she'd go to the prom with me.

"Come on. Sit here, son."

Mom patted the seat of the chair next to her. I scooted it until I was up against her elbow. Mom's cursive was elegant, full of soft, easy curves that slightly leaned to the right. I watched the formation of each letter. It couldn't be mistaken for anything other than the penmanship of a highbrow lady.

"You'll need a haircut, new shoes, and a tuxedo."

Mom pushed the pencil as if she were working on a major assignment.

"We can't forget the flowers for Mariah either," she said.

Toby cast his shadow over Mom's notepad. With his spider-leg finger, he pointed at each item she listed on the blue lines. I gave him the get-your-butt-back-into-that-chair look. Mom knew I didn't want him in my business. It puzzled me why she kept him around and included him in everything we did. If that wasn't enough, Grandma popped up at my side.

"Tell me about this gal you've been talking about," she said.

Grandma sure knew how to ask the big ones.

DUNKER

I thought for a minute, before I said, "Mariah's tall, almost as tall as me."

"And?" Grandma asked.

"Her feet are fast. She dribbles a ball, good as most of the guys on my team. She's got solid hands and sharp eyes, too. If I pass the ball to Mariah, she catches it, moves in, and sets the *pill* up just right. She can even make a shot from half-court. When Mariah gets the ball, she gets the points. She's a one-of-a-kind ball handler. There's not a guy I know who wouldn't pick Mariah to be on his Chickasaw Park team. Grandma, she's all right."

"Um-hum," Grandma said. "Is she a good girl? Makes good grades? Is she pretty? Can she dance? Is she Christian?"

I sighed and turned my head to not look at Grandma, but she got in my face anyway. She put her head close to mine and manhandled my chin.

"I don't want you keeping company with the wrong kind."

"Yes, Ma'am."

"Daughter, do you know this girl Dunker's

taking to the prom? And her family?"

"She's a lovely girl, Mother. Smart and very pretty. Her family lives not far from here. She and Dunker have been friends and classmates for some time. We know her family very well."

"I thought I said all that, Mom."

Grandma used her pointer and middle finger to bless herself. She punctuated her forehead. "In the name of the Father." Her fingers dropped to her chest. "And the Son." They crisscrossed her body, tapping both shoulders. "And the Holy Ghost. Amen."

After Grandma exaggerated the sign of the cross, I turned my attention back to Mom, who gave the notepaper to Dad and reminded him again about my haircut.

"And a shave," I blurted.

Mom gave me a look that no young man wanted. "I'm not going to pay to cut what I can't see," she said through pulled-tight lips.

I leaned back and gave Mom her space. I accepted the fact that she was going to let me grow old without a shave. How will I explain the *nubbies* on my face to Mariah? I can see her stroking my cheeks and jumping back to look at the abrasions on her fingertips.

My eyes flitted back and forth from Mom to Dad. I gnawed nervously on a toothpick that I'd picked up off the kitchen counter. I chewed it to a soft, woody mush, and could swallow it if I had the mind to. I was hoping Dad had a better understanding of this matter.

5

Paper Dolls
Delilah

Monday, leading up to prom day, Mariah browsed the periodical racks before she pulled a ton of magazines down to the floor: Brides, Teen Fashions, Bubble Gum Girl, Sweet Sixteen, and Girls' Summer Wear. She scanned them until she selected two that wouldn't be Mama's picks. The models featured on one cover flashed more skin than clothes. One licked a purple lollipop the size of her face. The model next to her posed with her legs further apart than Mama would consider decent. The beachgoer on the second cover wore a two-piece, pink and white, gingham swimsuit. She balanced a beach ball on her head and pushed her hip too far to one side. That's not good.

Mariah paid for the magazines. I didn't bother to warn her about her picks. It was too hot and too sticky to exchange words with her.

Back home, Mariah grabbed a pair of scissors, shoved everything aside, and plopped the magazines on the kitchen table. She flipped through them as if she were on a treasure hunt. She cut out models, turned them into paper dolls, and lined them up in front of her. I'd never seen Mariah give such attention to anything, not even her schoolwork when she wanted to impress Mama or one of her teachers.

"Whatcha doin', Mariah?"

"Scram! You make me sick."

Mariah scooped up the magazines, paper dolls, and scissors. She clutched them to her chest and dashed up the stairs. I followed her to make sure she didn't lose her mind along the way. She slammed the bedroom door, almost smashing my nose.

I turned the doorknob carefully. To not upset her, I eased into the room. Mariah was on the floor with the magazines scattered in front of her.

"Get out of here, or I'll tear those lips of yours off the front of your face if you don't. Gosh! You're the biggest pain in the world. Let me alone or I'll . . ."

I ducked out of the room before Mariah got up off the floor. This time, I slammed the door. I hurried back down the stairs, stunned because there was no reason for her to be annoyed with me.

Mariah pounced on her bed so hard, I covered my head to protect it from the plaster I thought was gonna fall from the ceiling. I didn't think my itty-bitty-teeny-weeny words would light her firecracker mind. But these days no one knew what to expect.

"Was that Mariah making a fuss?" Mama asked.

"Yep. That was her."

"What have you done, Delilah?"

"Nothing, Mama. Mariah's bent out of shape. She's turned herself into an oversized pretzel for no reason. I just wanted to ask her what she was looking for in those magazines. I promise you. That's all. No more. No less. I don't really care what she's looking for."

DUNKER

"Let your sister alone until this prom is over or, little miss, you'll be cleaning stalls at Churchill Downs until your prom day. The thoroughbreds will love you."

"Oh! Mama."

I got lost. I didn't want any of those strange punishments that Mama dishes out. I can hear her saying, "Read a book; weed the garden; wash the dishes for her or for Mrs. Donell, our sick neighbor across the street." And worst, iron a dress for Mariah. That kills me every time.

I kept myself busy training Beek, my normal gray Cockatiel with a yellow head, to say pretty girl and to call Frisk, our buff and white Shih-Tzu that I taught to jump through a hula hoop and rollover.

Tuesday, the doorbell rang. I looked toward the stairs to ensure that the coast was clear. I didn't want to be shoved aside by Mariah. Ever since this prom stuff started, she wouldn't let me answer the door. When I saw she was nowhere to be seen, I raced to the living room. I saw Dunker through the picture window. He sucked on his bottom lip while he squeezed his baseball cap and straightened his shirt. Sad. Sad. Sad. I opened the door wide and smiled big.

"Hi, Dunker. Come on in."

I stepped back so that he could. Frisk yapped and scratched at Dunker's leg.

"What's up, little sis? Mariah home?"

"She's here. Come on in. Have a seat."

I pointed toward the living room and refocused my attention toward the steps.

"Mariah." I waited before I belted her name the second time. "Mariah!" She still didn't answer. I sucked in a chest full of air and let it rip, "Maaa-Riii-Ahhh!"

"What do you want?"

Singing slow like, I drew his name out. "Dunker's here."

I went back to check on Dunker. He hadn't moved. He was still standing where I left him, looking as if he were going back out of the door. I leaned my head back and looked up into his nostrils. Sometimes, boogers were in them. Today they were clean. To impress Mariah, I bet.

DUNKER

"You want to sit down?"

Dunker followed me with a jock's walk that was slightly pigeon-toed and bouncy. I pointed to the sofa. "Go ahead. Sit there."

I was back in the foyer and sitting on the step, butted against the wall. That way Mariah won't bump me when she comes down the stairs. I glanced up just in time to see her descend the steps. She did a foot-to-foot as she bobbed her head. The girl reminded me of one of Cousin Jake's marionettes. That might be what's making her brain dizzy.

"Move out, trouble, or I'll squish you," Mariah said and bashed my shoulder with her left knee.

"Back to you," I said and poked the back of her knee with my fingernail, letting her know that I wouldn't be pushed around.

"Ouch," Mariah cried.

She shot me a fire-blasting look as she staggered to recover her balance.

"You better scram."

"You long, tall, splintered, clothesline prop. I'll dress you up in Mama's wash."

Judith C. Owens-Lalude

Mariah irked me. It was a good thing that Dunker was in the living room or the fight would be on. Except, Mama didn't allow us to misbehave when we had company, not even when it was Dunker.

Mariah was a giraffe on point when she crossed the room. And that wasn't cute. She sat down next to Dunker as if she were the Queen of the Jungle, but I knew better. She cozied up to him. They laughed at the nonsense they created and didn't make sense to me.

I eased across the step and butted my head against the stair rails for a better look. Dunker rested his arm on the back of the couch and adjusted himself to be closer to Mariah. He relaxed his arm so that it draped over her shoulder. Now, she was crammed up in his armpit. I hoped the hairs had stink bugs clinging to them.

Because Mama's wingback chair blocked part of my view, it was get-off-the-step time. I needed to know what Mariah and Dunker would do next.

I wiggle-wormed across the foyer on my belly, pulling with my fingers and pushing with my toes. I moved like a giant tortoise. Very discreetly, I grabbed one of the legs on the telephone bench and pushed it against the wall. I stood on the telephone book nook but still couldn't see what I wanted to see. So, I climbed on the back of the bench. Standing as tall as I could, I braced my body against the wall. I goosenecked around the molding until Mama's bench collapsed beneath, sending me rolling across the floor and landing on my back. Mariah and Dunker stood over me.

Mariah towered over me screaming, "What are you doing?"

Dunker's eyes bulked, his jaw lay low, and his lips struggled to move.

Back on my, feet I mumbled, "Just wanted to see if you and Dunker wanted something to drink," and hurried out of the room almost passing myself along the way. I'm not sure how much long Dunker stayed after that. I hid in the closet praying that Mariah wasn't angry with me and wouldn't tell Mama what I did. I didn't want one of Mama's never-ending lectures. Even though she wasn't in here with me, I heard her snapping voice ask, Who broke my telephone bench? What did I tell you about getting in your sister's way? Didn't I tell you to take care of your own business and leave Mariah to hers? Do you want to be grounded, or better yet, cleaning those stalls for a year? Young Lady!

    I stayed in the closet bunched in the dark corner, behind the coats, until I was sure Mariah had cooled off and Mama had no interest in me.

6

Uptown
Delilah

The Wednesday before prom day, Mama and Mariah shopped for a suitable dress. As usual, I had to tag along. Mariah selected several fancy gowns from the racks along the wall. In a lavender, baby doll dress with a shawl collar and gathered skirt, she slowly spun her body around.

"This is pretty, Mama, but I want to try them all on before I make my final decision."

Mariah stepped out of it and into a light-blue mini not much longer than Daddy's dress shirt.

"Much too short," Mama said.

Mama crossed her legs at the ankle and clutched the purse she balanced on her knees. Mariah didn't seem to notice Mama's disgust. She just pulled two more dresses off the rack. She wiggled into a yellow satin tube dress that barely brushed her ankles and looked at Mama.

"It's tight, dear. There's too little in the front and not enough in the back. And, it's blinding me."

Mama laid the back of her hand across her brow, pushing her eyeballs up 'til the dark brown of them nearly disappeared. She twisted and untwisted the soft handles on her purse while patting her foot.

My pest of a sister flounced a floor-length, leaf-green gown with at least fifty layers of ruffling. She spread the skirt with gestures equal to a peacock flaunting his tail feathers. Mariah admired it before she pulled it over her brainless head.

"How about this one, Mama?"

Mariah did a pirouette, kind of turn, followed by a curtsy.

"Pin a red-rose corsage on it and you'll be a big, fat, green salad. It doesn't matter what you wear to the prom. You can't dance," I told her.

Mama sighed with her eyes closed. She tried

to evaporate behind the lids.

"Mama, I'm gonna wait outside," I said.

On the sidewalk in front of the dress shop, I did the Candy-Cane Twist, snapped my fingers, and spun on my heels showing off my moves to the passersby. That is until Mama and Mariah came out. Mariah carried an oversized, glossy, white box with a pink ribbon tied around it and topped with a puffy bow. She pranced toward the car with a Cheshire cat grin. She's so far gone, she'll never find her way back to normal.

Mama unlocked the trunk of the car and pushed Mariah's dirty basketball stuff aside. She covered the floor with the clean rags bunched in front of her. Mariah sat the box down on them as if it contained Mama's fine china. I jumped in front of Mama, grabbed the trunk door, and slammed it. Mama was too slow.

"You beast! You almost smashed my fingers," Mariah grumped as she jumped back.

"Same to you," I said.

I walked behind Mama and Mariah. We

sauntered down the street to a Lady's Shoe Shop. We entered and sat three across in blond, bent wooden chairs. I was between Mariah and Mama. Mariah's arms layered both of her armrests. She gave me a butt-hole look, so I turned toward Mama and used her armrest.

"What's up, pretty ladies?" the shopkeeper asked.

Mariah grinned ear-to-ear as if he were speaking directly to her. Mama tightened her lips. She didn't approve of fresh talk from the young men, but let it pass, this time. He was lucky she didn't give him a young-man-you-should lecture. Instead, Mama went on to explain that Mariah needed a pair of prom shoes. He smiled, measured Mariah's feet and disappeared into a back room. He returned with an armload of shoeboxes. Only the crown of his head could be seen. He sat the load down and seated himself on the fitting stool in front of Mariah. He removed her basketball shoes and slid a pair of pumps onto her wiggly feet.

Mama told Mariah, "Those heels are too high. Those are too wide. Those are too low. Those heels are too . . ."

"I'll be outside, Mama."

I sat on the sidewalk next to the door under the awning and waited in the shade. I walked my thumbs and my index fingers, doing the itty-bitty-bug thing, 'til Toby came along.

"What's up, Delilah?"

"Oh, not much. Mama's buying Mariah a pair of prom shoes. And Mariah can't even dance."

"She can't! What are they gonna do at the prom?" Toby asked.

"Don't know. Sit and gawk at each other, I guess. They were all hugged up when Dunker came by the house to see her." Delilah said.

"I think they're on to each other. My brother told Sly on the telephone how good-looking and straight-up-sugar Mariah is."

"He wouldn't be saying those things if he lived at our house."

"Guess we better keep an eye on them. See you later. Gotta go. Come by the house if you can. I want to show you my new scooter."

Toby took off on his old homemade scooter. He leaned with it, too. After he turned and looked back at me, he raised his arm and waved so long.

"Cool!" I muttered.

I watched Toby's back as he moved down the street.

"Um-hum. Cute, cute, cute. Toby and the scooter. Sure wish he was in my same grade."

When he was out of sight, I went back to waiting and wondering what was going on with Mariah and Mama. The sidewalk underneath me suddenly felt hard. My butt ached, and it was ready for me to get off of it. I stood just as they came out of the shop. Mama was behind Mariah who skipped past me singing a tune I'd never heard, on or off the basketball court.

I pulled Mama aside. "Is that girl okay? She's got that funny color around her eyes again. Not to mention, she's doing that long-legged rag doll walk that I told you about. She's talking funny, too. Mama, she's losing it."

"Don't worry yourself about Mariah. You'll

understand when your prom day comes."

Mariah put the shoes in the trunk with the dress. She climbed into the backseat if you can believe that. Singing to herself, she studied whatever she saw out of the window.

Looking straight at Mama, I lowered my voice. "She's losing it," I said again. "I'm not sure how much longer I can tolerate her. She's getting stranger every day."

Mama gave me the shut-your-mouth eye. I slumped in my seat and stared out of the window until we got home. When Mama pulled to the curb, Mariah pushed the back of my seat forward to climb out.

"You're killing me. Hold on," I hollered.

When Mama opened the trunk of the car, Mariah rushed to get the dress box out. She scrambled up the sidewalk and went straight to our bedroom. "Stay away from me," she hollered from over her shoulder.

"I'm not interested in any old prom dress. If I wanted to, I could have my own," I shouted from the bottom step.

"Delilah, find something to keep yourself busy, or trouble will find you. Better yet, why don't you get something to eat and go to bed? You have school tomorrow."

Mama must be tired. It's still daylight outside and I have homework to do.

When Mariah came back downstairs, Mama refocused her attention on her and forgot about me.

"Don't forget, I'll pick you and Delilah up after school tomorrow. We have to drop off the shoes to be tinted and select a boutonniere for Dunker."

Mama spoke to Mariah in a much calmer voice than she had with me. They chatted as if I wasn't in the room. Mama prefers Mariah to me and I can't figure out why. Mariah's so out of sorts, she could be the lost piece of a jigsaw puzzle that didn't fit.

Thursday, prior to prom day, was hot and muggy. The sky was full of dark, threatening clouds so low they were a concern. I crossed the bluegrass lawn that separated our schools. When my feet touched down on

DUNKER

its cushiness, it felt like I was running on a deep shag carpet. I sat underneath the shade of the Red Maple Tree and tossed up tadpole-shaped seedpods that whirlybird back down.

When I glanced up, Mariah was heel-toeing her way down the sidewalk. She stretched her neck and shifted her eyes, but it wasn't me she was looking for. I parked myself in our usual meeting place and Mariah knew where that was. I hoped she'd find what she was searching for.

She stopped smack in front of me. "See Mama yet?" she asked, looking up and down the street instead of at me.

Mariah sat on the high, stonewall that framed the schoolyards. It followed the walkway for two blocks in both directions. She rubbernecked and waved to everyone who passed her.

"Who's that?"

"Somebody in my class," she said time after time.

"Can't be that many people in your class. Unless your classes are held in the gym. Hehehe."

Judith C. Owens-Lalude

Mariah hopped up on the yard wall to take advantage of the shade. She never stopped waving at her classmates.

Mama drove close to the curb in front of us and stopped. Mariah vaulted off the wall. She was in the front seat in nothing flat. She almost sat on the shoebox Mama had placed on the passenger seat. As hard as I could, I pushed the back of the front seat forward. I tried to smash Mariah as I slid in behind it.

There was no need to protest. Mama had said that my sitting in the backseat was fair because Mariah was older. That's okay. Mariah can have the front seat. Mama will see how far off the mountaintop Mariah is.

"Delilah, how did you do on your spelling test?"

"Mama, it was hard."

"Sounds as if you didn't do well. We'll talk more when we get home. You were warned."

I scooted down in my seat, glad Mariah was thinking about something that had her staring out of the window and not teasing me about my spelling test. Which is what she did whenever Mama scolded me about it.

At Kobi's Cobbler Shop, Mariah got out of the car doing a two-step with a skip. I kept a safe distance to allow the much-needed oversized gap between us. That's what a crazy person requires.

"You need to give it up, girl," I said, sharing my unwanted advice with her.

"Forget'cha," she said.

Mariah knew I was behind her and let the shop door shut in my face. That would have been dangerous if Mama wasn't with us.

"I want these tinted cloud-pink, please," Mariah said to the help behind the counter and danced out of the shop.

I wanted to clip her heels, but Mama was behind us and would have scolded me.

Afterward, we trotted to the flower shop a few doors down from the shoe shop. On the way, Mama and Mariah chitchatted about prom stuff. The cowbell rang as we opened the redwood, framed, glass door.

Judith C. Owens-Lalude

The florist smiled, "Can I help, you?"

"I'd like to get a perfect, pink, rose boutonniere without spots on the flowers."

"What is your color preference for the ribbon?"

"Purple and green," Mariah said and turned abruptly without giving the florist an opportunity to show her the ribbon samples and didn't offer a thank you or a please.

Mariah and I were out the door, but Mama stayed behind to clean up the mess Mariah exhibited with her bad behavior. Mama made the ribbon selections from a bunch of streamers. I'm sure she expressed her gratitude to the shopkeeper for his kind assistance.

Mariah nearly knocked Mr. Bell down, the blind beggar, when she came out of the shop. I felt so bad that I teased my buffalo nickel out of my pocket that I saved to buy a peppermint stick. I dropped it in his tin cup. "Thanks," Mr. Bell said when it click-clacked on the bottom of his cup. I felt good and didn't miss the nickel.

Mariah reclaimed the front seat, forcing me to the rear. As usual, I was the rejected child. There was no use making a fuss. Mama was still in the Mariah's-important mode.

When Mama drove off, the wind from the open windows blew my bangs straight up. My braids whipped my eyelashes. I collapsed in my seat to keep the plaits under control. Mariah wouldn't have rolled her window up if I had asked her to. She was busy being totally tuned into herself. If Daddy were here, he wouldn't tolerate such unfavorable treatment of me. He always said that I was his special child. When we got home, I went my way and stayed there until it was time to go to the beauty parlor on Friday.

That day, Miss Pearl's shop was crammed with prom queens. It seemed as if every senior girl in town was there. Mama went in with us because she wanted my hair washed and I didn't have an appointment. I would have to be worked on between the scheduled customers.

"I'll take care of the girls. You go on home. I'll call when they're done," Miss Pearl told Mama.

"Delilah, behave yourself. I don't want any trouble out of you."

Judith C. Owens-Lalude

It was sometime later before Miss Pearl was bent over the shampoo bowl, lathering Mariah's head. Afterward, Mariah was put under a dryer that hummed as it bellowed out hot air.

Miss Thelma, the manicurist who was only in the shop during holidays and special occasions, wheeled a small manicure table from one customer to the next. As far as I could tell, she hadn't changed much since Christmas. She was still short, skinny, and knot-kneed. Today she wore a powder-blue, button-up, notched collar blouse with rolled-up sleeves, near to her shoulders. The tail of it was tucked into the waistband of a straight, midnight-blue skirt, belted at the waist. Her penny strollers were polished and had brand-new Lincoln pennies tucked into the slots.

"Would you care to have your nails done while you're under the dryer?" Miss Thelma asked Mariah.

Mariah didn't hear her. Miss Thelma tilted her head and spoke up into the hot air. That's when Mariah positioned her hands on the tabletop.

"Yes, please."

"And the color?"

"Strawberry Pink, please."

After I was shampooed, I watched the seven hairdressers and wondered what it'd be like if I were one of them. They each had a styling station along the walls with baby pictures taped on the mirrors. Miss Pearl's salon table was set off to the side by itself. Her big mirror, twice the size of theirs, was filled with photographs of older family member and babies on tricycles and some in strollers.

Straightening combs cling-clanged the burners when they were laid between the twin rows of tiny holes bellowing out yellow-tipped blue flames. Before they were shoved into the hair near the scalps of the girls, they were dragged across a white towel to ensure they weren't overheated. They usually left behind scorch marks from the teeth. With a twist of the wrist and pump of the arm, the beauticians drew the hot combs toward their chests. The oil sizzled, sending up a smoke-laced aroma of oiled hair.

Their arms pumped, pulling the kinky hair straight until it could be compared to black silken threads stretched on a loom. All the hot combs and

curling irons in the shop clanged a rhythmic beat–
Click-clack-click. Click-clack. Click-click. Beauty
music, Mama called it. Next, the Marcella irons were
heated up. Holding onto the handles with the prongs
open, the beauticians clamped onto the ends of the
hair and repeatedly turned them until they were right
at the scalp. There was no mistaking the sweet smell of
beauty generated in the shop.

Prom head after prom head was filled with
rows of shiny, black Marcella curls the size of my
little finger lined up military-style, but not styled to
preserve them for prom night.

Prom-goers left the shop two and three at a
time. I wanted to leave after my hair was washed,
nearly two and a half hours ago and I'm still here.

Finally, Miss Pearl telephoned Mama. She
let her know that we were almost ready. I was at the
window monitoring the traffic when Mama drove past
the shop. She didn't stop; she circled the block. After
the third lap, she double-parked in front of Miss
Pearl's. I ran out to greet her.

"Where's your sister?"

DUNKER

"She's coming. She's got a little more time in the chair."

I was about to jump in the car, when Mama said, "Go wait with your sister while I circle the block again."

By the time Mama returned, Miss Pearl and Mariah were coming out of the shop. Mariah was prancing. She was being Miss *It* or something. I'm not sure what. Mariah butted me with her hip to be first in the car.

"Move it, or I'll be on you with a whack that you won't forget," she said.

I ducked, darted past her, and jumped in the front seat. I wasn't going to be bullied. Mama gasped and I went over the back of the seat to my assigned spot. The right side of Mama's face could be seen in the rearview mirror if she peered into it or glanced over her right shoulder. That was good because when she did, I could give her a warning glare when Mariah was about to lose the rest of her mind.

"Sorry for taking so long with your girls, Mrs. Bentley. We had a lot of last-minute prom heads to do.

Gotta go. Come back and see me soon."

"Thank you, Pearl, for taking care of my girls."

"My pleasure."

Mariah and Mama were so quiet and caught up in their thoughts, that they didn't notice Miss Pearl waving good-bye to them. The hush in the car made the drive home more agreeable for me. I wondered why there was so much fuss being made about the prom. It wasn't like it was Christmas Eve and Santa was on his way to our house with gifts. Proms came and went quickly and no toys or candy-stuffed stockings were left behind.

Mama parked the car in front of the house. Mariah was challenged when she had to open the car door and not bump her freshly polished nails. She fanned her fingers out and arrogantly swayed her hands this way and that. I slid across the seat and got out on the driver's side of the car. To be nice, I went around to open the door for Mariah. Otherwise, she would've been in there 'til the Death Valley hot springs bubbled up ice cubes.

"Close your mouth and come on, girl. If you don't hurry up, I'll leave you on the other side of this door."

Once inside the house, Mariah sat at the kitchen table, hands extended, wiggling them at whomever was near. That was me. Frisk strolled past us and showed no interest in Mariah's nails. Beek was hunkered down in the back of his cage and didn't come up to note the goings-on. Mariah flexed her wrist as if she wanted me to kiss the back of her hand. That would be a comic book scene.

"I'm not sure this prom thing's good for you."

Mariah huffed, "Where's Daddy?"

"Didn't you see him with Mama when we got out of the car? They went to pick up your prom shoes and flowers."

Mariah started fiddling with the curls on her head. Bobby pins dropped to the floor one at a time.

"Oh! No! You gotta help me."

"Okay! Okay! What's wrong with you, Mariah? I'm only in the sixth grade and I know you can't do anything with freshly painted nails. Besides, you need to put a stopper in those eye sockets of yours or you're gonna drown yourself."

"If I don't get my curls pinned or rolled back up, my head's gonna be an ugly mess tomorrow. You gotta help me!"

"I'm trying. Sit still. And keep your hands away from your head."

"Where are you going?"

"I'll be back."

I grabbed a brown paper bag and ripped it into narrow strips. I twisted each piece into brown-paper kits. When done, I stretched the curls, one at a time; rolled each on a kit down to the scalp; and tied the twisties to hold them in place.

7

Two Points
Delilah

The next morning, I peered into the bed next to me. The long-legged monster was still sleeping. Quiet as a mound of whipped cream tumbling on its side, I went downstairs to eat breakfast alone. That was good. I wouldn't have to look at Mariah more than necessary. Wanting to go outside to check the weather, I hurried to finish my eggs and cinnamon toast.

Rested against the foundation of the house, I fiddled with my uncombed braids. I thought about the day that Dunker asked Mariah to the prom. It was Thursday, the 26th of May, 1969. I remember because I had one of those tough spelling tests that day and didn't do well on it either.

Mama put me and my desk in the time-out corner. That's when the hall phone rang. It was Dunker calling. He wanted Mariah to play ball with him the next day after school. She knew that she couldn't beat him fairly. After all, he got the nickname, Dunker, because he was the major slammer on the team, just not the star player. Dunker could dribble the ball with one hand or two, palm it, leap into the air, and slam dunk the pill.

Mariah and I went to the park early that day. Dunker popped the big question to her. I waited patiently on the bench for her to finish practicing her free throw shots. I remembered trying to get her attention because I was hungry, tired, and wanted to go home. I had homework to do. That's when Dunker came over the hill with a black eye.

"Hey, little sis, what's up?" he asked me.

"Not much," I told him.

Dunker fidgeted with his satchel strap, confused and seeming not to know what to do with his hands, unusual for him. He had the steadiest hands on the team. He shot air hoops even when he didn't have a ball or a basket.

Mariah saw Dunker and stopped dribbling. She turned three different shades of brown. When her natural chestnut color returned, she called out to him. Dunker set his bag down and trotted out to the center court. Mariah used an overhead pass to put the ball in play. Dunker fumbled, retrieved it, and started a rapid hand-to-hand dribble before he passed the ball back and forth between his legs–pure showmanship.

"Come on, come on, give it up, Dunker," Mariah said and flailed her limbs to block his shot.

Dunker's javelin-long left arm went up against her guard while he managed the ball with his right hand. When he was settled, he raised the ball above his head. With his feet parted and his shoulders square, he bent his knees and took in a breath so deep his ribs showed through the soggy shirt that clang to them. Dunker went up feet off the ground for the long shot, but when he eyed Mariah, he missed the shot and came down bobbing on one foot. Mariah nabbed the rebound, bounced the ball, squat-turned, and went for the layup.

"Two points," she gloated.

I could see, Dunker was stupefied by what happened, but he caught the ball when it came off the rim. Mariah pushed her plaits back off of her face. With her elbows angled outward, she grinned, flashing her teeth at him. Dunker sucked in his bottom lip. dribbled in for what he intended to be a smooth layup shot, but instead, the ball hit him in the face. He missed the play and landed at Mariah's feet. The guy's nervous, I thought. Mariah stumbled backward, nearly falling, but didn't. However, she stole the ball, swung around, and sprang up for a hoop.

"Two points," she bragged.

Mariah wouldn't ease up. Dunker was back in her circle with both hands up. He was a snowball demon moving and melting. Suddenly he stopped in mid-play.

"Enough of this. I need to ask you something," he said, loud enough for me to hear. Dunker clutched Mariah's upper arm. "Let's go. We need to talk," he

DUNKER

said and pulled her along.

Mariah glared at me. I rolled my eyes. I was the three wise monkeys bundled into one–hear no evil, see no evil, speak no evil.

Mariah and Dunker trudged to the far end of the court. From underneath the basketball net, they gawked at each other. Whatever he had to say, he'd better be swift. Mama was waiting for us and I was tired, hot, and hungry.

I drew my knees up and rested my head on them, but raised it when Dunker hooked his arm around my sister's neck. I thought, he's eating out of her ear or drooling in it. If it's full of wax, it'd serve him right. Mariah had no business under that basket with a boy. What could be that important?

I watched them with my spying eyes. Mama would want to know about this. Why couldn't Dunker stand up straight and talk like regular folk? Now, Mariah was bobbing her head. She even batted her eyelashes. Strange. She's changed colors again and her feet are turned in. The toes on her right foot flirted with the ones on her left one.

"That's it! Let's go! It's almost dark." I yelled. "And Mama's waiting for us."

If anyone else was in the park, they heard me, too. Except, we seemed to be the only people there that day.

Mariah flipped around. She skipped like a drunkard toward me. The girl must be possessed by a demon, I thought.

As soon, as we started our walk home, I could tell Mariah's mind was someplace else. I walked next to her with my head down and my hands clasped behind me. I kicked a rock down the sidewalk when what came out of my mouth was, "You'd better stop that prancing. You know what Mama told you. What's up with you and Dunker anyway? He was hanging all over you . . . in your ear and stuff."

Mariah shrugged her shoulders, rolled her eyes, and swung her crooked braids at me. She shoved her nose up so high, I hoped a big, fat, American Robin pooped in both her nostrils.

"You look sick. What's wrong with you, girl?"

"What makes you think something's wrong with me?"

"You're green."

Mariah hunched her shoulders and did a skip-step. She cut in front of me and zigzagged back and forth down the sidewalk, nearly falling off the curb. I hoped Mama could do something for her when we got home.

Mariah pushed open the front door, stepped inside, and stood in the center of the foyer. Her eyes scanned the ceiling as if a monkey was swinging on the light fixture, or something. The next thing I knew, she was hugging her stinky body. In a snap, she stretched her arms, palms up. She looked as if she were worshiping the *God of Ceilings*. I doubt that *He* wanted to be bothered. She was a goner. When Frisk saw her, he tucked his tail and scooted underneath the wingback chair in the living room.

"You okay, Mariah?" Mama asked, trying to understand the strange animal that was loose in the house.

"Yeah, Mama. Guess what?" Mariah sighed,

Judith C. Owens-Lalude

moaned, swooned, and sighed again. "Dunker asked me to go to the prom with him."

Now, Mariah was spinning out of control. She was a runaway tire going downhill.

"How nice, dear. What did you say?"

Mama started to relax a bit, but her eyes never stopped studying Mariah.

"Is that what this is all about?" I asked.

"Mind your own business!" Mariah said.

My sister was so lit up, she could've been a Halloween luminary.

"You can't go to the prom. You don't know how to dance. All you can do is play ball."

"I can learn."

Mariah rolled her eyes, twirled, and batted her eyelashes. Good thing she's got shorts on. A skirt would've been over her head. She stopped, glanced at me, held her head to one side, and wasted no time rushing off to our bedroom.

"Mama, we gotta talk. The girl's in trouble. What's she gonna do at the prom? She can't dance!"

"Don't worry, Delilah. We'll teach her.

DUNKER

By the way, how was your test today? Did you get a passing grade?"

"Mama, my teacher said I got a lot of room for improvement."

"You can start now. Push your desk over to that corner. I'll let you know when dinner's ready."

By the time Mama remembered me, dinner was over. I watched her and Mariah sitting at the kitchen table. They listed prom things like dresses, hairstyles, shoes, fingernails, make-up, and flowers. Girly words that made *goop* hang in the air. Because of their chattering, I couldn't think about the things I needed to think about.

"Make your hair appointment now, Mariah," with an intense glance she said, "be quick and get your dinner and sit down."

I fixed myself a plate and ate alone. I was an abandoned child without a family. Mariah sprang from her chair. She dashed down the hall in her sock feet and nearly broke her leg when she glided into the telephone table. She shamed Willie Mays' slide into third base.

"Drat," Mariah cried.

Judith C. Owens-Lalude

She was a body heap on the floor, rubbing her shin and holding back tears. When they dropped, she pushed them away with the short sleeve of her blouse and picked up the headset to dial the beauty shop's telephone number. When the ring stopped, I knew Miss Pearl picked up her headphone. "Pearl's Beauty Shop," she said.

Mariah sniffled into the phone. "Please, Miss Pearl. Can't you squeeze me in? Just this once, Miss Pearl. Please! Please!"

Mariah dragged her voice out so, I almost cried. She never begged like that even when she wanted money to buy new sneakers when her old ones were still doing their job. Mariah hung up the phone. She pulled herself up off the floor and strut-skipped back to Mama.

"Got an appointment with Miss Pearl for Prom Friday. She said she'll have to work me in. Sure glad she didn't say no. What would I've done?"

I remember how mad I was at myself when I almost felt sorry for Mariah boohooing those crocodile tears into the telephone.

Enough thinking. It's too hot and humid out

here, and I need to get dressed. I went back around the house to the kitchen door. It was still unlocked. I let myself in. If Mariah had known I was outside she would have flipped the door latch and locked me out, yelling for help.

8

Barbershop Blues
Dunker

On Friday, Prom Eve, school was dismissed early for the seniors. The cowbell at *MR. CUTS* rang when Dad and I entered the shop. It was hot and packed with prom people. I was light-headed and queasy. Glancing around the shop, I noticed two rows of six black vinyl chairs, each set, front to front with an oblong table between the rows. The chairs were chrome-trimmed, with gauze-stuffed seats oozing foam from the cracks. It was evident they had cradled countless rear-ends. The beauty shops didn't have such overused, raggedy furnishings. Mom and Grandma always talked about how nice and comfortable the chairs were at Miss Pearl's beauty shop.

Dad and I sat in pair of empty chairs and waited for my turn with the barber. My mind couldn't concentrate on what came from the radio that belted out the latest hits. My thoughts were preoccupied with how much of Mariah I might be able to touch on prom day. I wondered, too, if she was sitting in one of those beauty shop chairs waiting to be transformed into her idea of beauty. I hoped she didn't change a thing about herself. She was too fine to be tampered with.

I was struggling to get my mind off of Mariah when the image of a basketball featured on a magazine cover appeared near the bottom of stacked periodicals. I decided to ease it out. I flipped through its pages, and looked but didn't see or read a thing.

"What's your pleasure today, Mr. Womack?"

I rolled the magazine into a baton and squeezed it as if I were choking the venom out of an enemy snake that had crawled into my space.

"How about a haircut and a shave for Raymond?" Dad said.

Dad nodded for me to go ahead and sit in the

barber's chair. I was about to embark on my début as a man. No more shaving with cardboard razors and fake soap behind closed doors or behind the backs of those who didn't believe I was ready for a shave.

Mr. Knobs, Dad's regular barber, was slightly tall and pear-shaped. His salt-and-pepper hairline receded toward the middle of his head. His handlebar mustache smiled when he did. He was the only Negro in town, I knew, that had that kind of mustache.

"Have a seat here," Mr. Knobs said, patting the back of the barber chair.

I dropped the rolled-up magazine on top of the yuck-stack. It toppled to the floor and disappeared beneath the chair. I pretended not to see what had happened and strolled over to the barber's chair. I slid into it with a purpose. With my feet braced on the footrest, I lowered my arms onto the popsicle-cold armrests. I did a few up-and-down moves until my forearms adjusted to the shock.

A button clicked. A motor revved. Clippers buzzed. Mr. Knobs pruned the crown of my head. He cropped the hairs on the top, sides, and rear. When he was done, he hit the off button and hung the clippers back on a hook. He lifted the trimmers from their catch. Taking his time, he let them glide across my neck, snipping and shaping my nape and sideburns. Mr. Knobs replaced them with the edger. The bumblebee buzz of them let me know that the haircut was nearing its end. Mr. Knobs swapped the trimmers for the edgers. He used them to create a sharp defining line as he nipped at the edges of my hairline. 'Shaping', the barbers called it. When Mr. Knobs was done, he hung the edger back on the hook next to the trimmers.

He fumbled through a whatnot drawer 'til he nabbed a pair of scissors. He came around to the front of me to study my head. Squeezing my temples between his pointer and long fingers, he anchored my forehead. Holding firm, he sheared off the straggly hairs that stood above the rest. Mr. Knobs had the same studying look on his face that Dad did whenever he trimmed Paco.

When Mr. Knobs put the scissors away, he reclined the back of the barber chair. My body felt heavy but calm. He wrapped my face with warm, wet towels. Highs and lows rippled through me, inside and outside. I was a carnival ride whose canopy just fell over it. The mucus in my sinuses loosened and dropped to the back of my throat. I choked, coughed, and swallowed hard to clear a pathway for better breathing.

"You okay, son?" Mr. Knobs asked.

I bobbed my chin to indicate an affirmative.

When Mr. Knobs poured hot water into the shaving mug, the aroma of spice indicated that it was Dad's cup kept there for his shaves. My ears snatched up the knocking sounds from the wooden brush handle against the cup. The clacking informed me that I was about to become the man that I wanted to be. I knew what followed the swashing of the bristles that lathered up the soap.

On my trips to the barbershop with Dad, when I was a little boy, I watched Mr. Knobs shave him. It was only a dream one day I would sit in this very chair that Dad had for his shaves. There was no cardboard razor or cup of pretend soap.

The chair reclined further. Now I was flat on my back. I looked up at the ceiling lights. When I did,

Mariah emerged; she stood in my daydream. As Mr. Knobs removed the towels from my face, *she peered down at me.* He slathered whipped shaving cream over my cheeks, chin, and under my nose. The smell was soothing. My eyelids grew heavy and closed out the overhead lights. The tightness in my muscles relaxed. They slowly released the hold they had on my bones.

Mariah draped her arms around my neck and held on. We swayed back and forth with the rhythm of the shaving blade that smacked against the leather razor strop fastened to the side of the barber chair.

When the blade stopped, the quiet alerted my ears. I wanted to open my eyes, but they were still held captive by the heaviness of their lids.

Mr. Knobs touched my nose. Startled, I pulled back.

"Sorry," he said and dragged the shaving blade along the underside of my chin and up toward my ears.

My body settled deeper into the comfort of the barber care. My mental sensors followed every movement of the blade. Mr. Knobs shaved the hairs from my face that Mom couldn't see. Trapped in the shaving cream, they were skimmed away leaving my cheeks slicker than an oil spill. When Mariah gets in my face, the way she does when she guards me on the court, she won't elbow me in the eye. She'll land a kiss on my polished cheeks. Oh, the joy!

Mr. Knobs mopped up the excess cream with one of the warm towels and splashed me with aftershave lotion. It stung, but that was okay. It would keep down the razor bumps. With a face smooth as a brand new puppy, Mariah will be eager to go cheek-to-cheek with me and maybe, do a little lip-locking.

Mr. Knobs raised the back of the barber chair. Using a soft brush, he dusted the back of my neck with talcum powder. Afterward, he swiveled the barber chair around and offered me a mirror. I reclaimed my legs and stood up. With my lips sucked in, I raised the mirror to see the rear of my head–pure art, clean and neat with well-defined lines.

"Boy! Oh, boy!"

"Is it to your liking?"

"It's all good."

I laid the mirror on the barber's bench. I stretched my arms, did an oversized yawn, and *gave Mariah the usual wink.* I strolled to where Dad stood. He paid Mr. Knobs and we left the shop. Dad gave me a slap on the back.

"Welcome to the man's world," he said and pulled out Mom's list. "No need to go back to the car. This way." Dad said, gesturing with his head in the direction we needed to go.

We were off to the tuxedo store down the street and around the corner. We walked and we talked. Dad was tall and slim, but not as tall or slim as me. We fell into a racer's stride that created a tempo that only professional walkers could top. I was glad we had the sidewalk to ourselves. Dad and I covered it with our sure-footedness. We didn't let up on our pace until we were at the tuxedo shop. When we entered, Mr. Kelly greeted us. He gave Dad a lost-and-found-buddy handshake.

"How ya doing, Kelly?" Dad asked. He seemed to know everyone in town.

"I'm fine. It's good to see you and the boy.

Come on in. Haven't seen Raymond since he was a little fella. Grown a lot since then."

Mr. Kelly, whose head was shoulder-high to me, drew his head back to contemplate what he might do for me. He waved me toward the showcase.

"Come on over here, Mr. Womack."

Mr. Kelly recognized my manhood. It must be the shave.

"You too, Dad."

Mr. Kelly went to work. Not saying more, he reached up and clasped my shoulders with his thick hands.

"You've gotta standstill."

He drew a length of mustard-colored tailor's tape down the center of my back, stopping at my waist. Next, he pressed the metal tip into my belly button and looped it around my waist.

"Thirty-one inches."

The tape was stretched down the inside and outside of my leg, to determine which length of pants would be best for me.

"Mum-hum."

With the toe of his shoe, he hooked the leg of a wooden stool and dragged it from beneath the counter. He stood on it and laid the tape measure across my chest. "Mum-hum," he mumbled again. Pushing my shoulders gently, he turned me to measure across my back, shoulder to shoulder, and the length of each arm.

"Mum-hum."

Mr. Kelly stepped down, pushed the stool back underneath the counter, and looped the tape measure around his neck. He supported his right forearm on the glass case to record the numbers on his tailor's tablet. His facial expressions were concerning.

When Mr. Kelly shifted his boxcar mustache from side to side, there was no remnant of a smile. After he scanned his figures, he picked up his notepad and disappeared behind a pair of black pleated drapes. My stomach sank.

Hiccup. Hiccup. Hiccup.

Dad gave me a grim look. "You okay, son?"

"Yeah, Dad."

This tuxedo business was too serious for me. The tape measure never made it from my waist to my ankle or wrist-to-wrist when my arms were stretched out airplane-wing style.

I stood at the center of the shop, not certain what to do. If there wasn't a tux that would fit me, I wouldn't be able to knock on Mariah's door. I had to look dapper. If I didn't, she wouldn't leave her house with me.

I fiddled with a box of ties. I rearranged cufflinks scattered on the showcase. I even tossed a few air hoops between hiccups. Time didn't know that I needed an answer, and needed it now—tux or no tux.

With my lips to Dad's ear, I said, "What are we gonna do if he doesn't . . . ?"

"Let's wait and see."

I hiccuped again, danced foot-to-foot, and bit at the inside of my cheek until I tasted blood.

Mr. Kelly finally came out of the stockroom. He gave me a serious glance. "Don't let this prom rattle you. Go ahead. Try this on."

I took the suit, walked over to the narrow changing room, and pushed open the café doors. I crouched to keep my fresh haircut out of the overhead light fixture, with a bulb so dim it didn't need to be there.

I toed off my old basketball shoes, stepped out of my sports shorts, and tugged on the cool black tuxedo trousers. They came up and over my hips without much fuss. When I straightened my back, a rush of dust showered me. I cursed the overhead light and pinched my nose to block an oncoming sneeze.

"Nice fit on these slacks."

"You okay, son? You sound strange."

"Yeah, Dad."

I pulled the suspenders up on my shoulders and let them go with a snap and fastened the cummerbund on top of them. I slid my arms into the jacket sleeves and jerked my shoulders to adjust it. I buttoned and unbuttoned it several times to assess the guy in the mirror. When I attempted to step back for a better view, I whacked the wall behind me.

"Feels good. Looks good, too," I said.

"Come on out. Let's make sure it's what you want," Dad said.

Two gorilla steps put me in front of Mr. Kelley's three-way mirror. I stood there in my sock feet, gawking past Dad, who stood between me and the mirror. He grinned and I skirted around him for a better glimpse at my reflection.

"Not bad. Not bad at all," I said.

Mariah was checking out this tall, brown, handsome guy, digging what she saw. There she is! Coming at me. I raised my arms to reach out to her.

"Sleeves okay, son?"

"They're fine, Dad."

I brought my arms down and gently placed my hands in the small of Mariah's back. I drew her close to me and dipped her over my arm. We glided into a slow turn, dancing to our private music.

I was raising her arm to swirl her when my body stiffened inside the tuxedo. The coat sleeves rose too far above the pointy bones of my wrists. I tugged on the hems of the sleeve and then drew in my gut and shook my legs to lengthen the pants that hovered above my ankles.

"Got a problem, son?"

"No, Dad. This suit's all right."

Mr. Kelly glanced at Dad. "Mr. Womack, that's the longest tuxedo I have."

"We'll take it," I said.

I disappeared behind the café doors. I didn't want anything more to be said. There was no need to negotiate for the tux. This was not the time to be finicky. My teammates, taller than me, didn't get formal wear.

I changed out of the tuxedo, threw it over the café doors, and got back into my street clothes. While I was stooped beneath the light fixture, that tried to fry my brains, Mr. Kelly was hooking the fastener of the purple and green paisley cummerbund onto the hanger with the white shirt. He tucked a matching bow tie and handkerchief into the jacket pocket and zipped everything up in a fancy garment bag.

"Thank you, Kelly," Dad said.

The weight of the tuxedo on the hangers pinched my fingers, but I didn't mind. I had a tuxedo. Sly and his shadows could cover the keyhole on the basketball court better than a fitted sheet on a mattress. But when it came to tuxedos, their arms and legs wouldn't let them come near to a proper fit.

Dad and I trotted back to the truck. I wondered what Mom would say about me renting a not-so-good-fitting tuxedo. I doubted she'd notice since she couldn't see the hairs on my face. Dad got in behind the wheel and rolled the window down on his side.

I stood at the rear of the truck. The cab was so cluttered with Dad's dirty odds and ends. I decided the tuxedo would ride up front with me. I settled down in the passenger seat and doubled it over on my lap. Dad's truck slow-rolled its way down the street. I leaned back and rested my eyes as my shoulders rose and fell with ease.

A hot breeze buffed my cheeks. *Mariah drew her fingertips down the back of my head.* My eyes opened to investigate what had just happened to me and to be sure of where I was. Dad was still behind the wheel, watching the road up ahead. He hummed one of those Motown hits. A few minutes later we were home.

"I'll see you in the house. Got to get back to

work, son."

"Dad! I still gotta get shoes."

"Tomorrow."

"That's prom day!"

"We'll shop early."

"It's gonna be all right," I said, reassuring myself.

Easy stepping, I maneuvered around Mom's flowerbeds. At the backdoor, I took in a gulp of the warm floral-scented air that wafted from the garden. Just when the sweet fragrance scented passed beneath my nose, something brushed my shoulder. I swung around. No one was there, except Mom's flowers mocking me. I stepped inside the summer-warm kitchen filled with Mom's cooking aromas. Today it was beef and gravy, sweet potato pie, and yeast rolls. Foods normally reserved for Sunday. Grandma was at the table bent over her catechism.

"Where's Dunker, honey?" Mom called to Dad from the living room,

"I'm here, Mom."

"My my, you look fresh and clean. Haircuts

seem to spruce you up."

Grandma couldn't get on her feet fast enough. She was in my face and patting my barbershop shave in record time. I flinched. She grinned at me. Mom did too. I shifted my eyes back and forth between the two of them. I wondered if they knew I had been shaved. I glanced at Dad. He winked. We had decided there was no need for them to know about all our barbershop business.

"Gotta go, Mom. See you later, Grandma."

Toby followed me to the steps. I didn't know where he had come from. I didn't see him when I came in the house and, now, he's polluting my space.

"Get off my heels, turd."

Halfway up the stairs, Toby was still behind me. I swung the garment bag to knock him back down the steps. He ducked.

"Hey! Watch it," he said and reached for the bag.

"Touch it and I'll rearrange your legs."

Toby raised his forearm to block the attack he

thought was coming.

"I ain't interested in your old stuff. Nobody but you wants to be a Loony Tune penguin wearing a tuxedo."

I held onto my suit. It was my *Trophy of the Day*. When I got to my room, Toby was still on my trail.

"Scram! I'm gonna slam dunk your butt in a way it won't come back up."

I kicked the door shut with the flat of my foot to close out Toby and the downstairs noise. I hung the tuxedo on the door hook with my bathrobe. Stretched out on the bed, I tucked my arms behind my head, crossed my legs, and studied the ceiling to block out the rest of the day.

9

If the Shoe Fits
Dunker

Mom wasn't in sight when I came back downstairs the next morning. She had gone to pick up the prom flowers, I heard her say so to Dad. Toby was out spending the day with Grandma, who was the only person who laughed at his sick jokes. 'Tell me again,' she'd say to him. Dad was slow-walking through the house, maybe, checking for what needed to be fixed.

"Let's go, Dad. Today's it. We get shoes, or I'm ice cream on a hot grill."

I rushed out of the door to clue Dad that it was time to move. I hurdled over the car door and dropped into the driver's seat; he did the same on the passenger's side. Dad was fun to chauffeur around town. He knew how to ride in a jalopy.

Mom would stand next to Blue and wait for me to open the door for her and close it, too. When we'd take off, she'd complain about the wind blowing her skirt up and sending her hat to the back of her head, or mussing up her hairdo. She'd even nag about the dirt and grease on the seat that couldn't be seen.

I took care of Big Blue, always making sure he was clean, polished, and top-of-the-line hot rod ready. That's the way he was when Grandaddy Hoss gave him to me.

After I parked Blue, Dad looked at his watch. "Got two hours, son."

I was the timekeeper. If we got back late, I had to pay Dad as if the meter timed out. Today, that wouldn't be good. I didn't have extra coins for Dad. I needed my money for the prom. Mariah was my queen and she deserved a king.

The cowbell announced to us as we entered the store. Dad and I were the first customers of the day. Mr. Greg, the shopkeeper was in a good-morning mood. He had an unassuming but pleasant smile when he greeted us.

He was a medium-built person with broad shoulders and dark skin. He had on a fresh pair of pressed khaki slacks, a blue oxford shirt, and a yellow polka-dotted tie that complemented his outfit. His oxblood, wingtip loafers were perfectly polished and matched the belt that he wore. I couldn't get that look if I tried, not even on a Sunday. The man's cool and smells good, too.

"Come on in. I'm Greg," he said.

Mr. Greg shook our hands. His eyes were bright and friendly. They blinked when he spoke.

"What can I do for you gentlemen?" he asked.

Ooh, wee! Knows how to talk, too.

"My son needs a pair of black dress shoes."

"Have a seat. Let's measure your feet."

When I sat down, Mr. Greg took one look at my feet and skipped the measuring. The truth was his equipment couldn't do the job. He went to the back of the shop and returned with an armload of shoeboxes.

After I shoved my feet into more pairs of shoes than I wanted to, I had it. My feet were too big, too stubborn, and didn't want to be squeezed into fancy, patent leather loafers. I sighed, kicked off the last pair, and slid my *dogs* back into my old faithfuls.

"These feel mighty good, Dad."

Dad thanked Mr. Gregg and we left.

"What do we do now, son?"

I looked at my watch. "We still got plenty of time. Let's try MR. HOOPS athletic store. It's only two blocks down the street."

"That's Batter Smith's shop, isn't it?"

"Yeah, he takes care of the team's needs. I'm sure he can fix me up with a pair of shoes that'll have my feet dancing the Chicago Walk when they ain't doing the Twist."

Dad grinned and we took off with our one-of-a-kind racers' stride. Dad's okay. Mom could never keep up with us.

At HOOPS' Dad glimpsed at me. "I hope we're at the right place," he said.

In his baritone, voice Mr. Smith said, "Come on in."

Judith C. Owens-Lalude

Although he was an older man with a Widow's Peak and heavy sideburns, the team members and I called him Mr. Batter. He was always around the locker room, helping us with our uniforms and fitting us with sports shoes.

Today, Mr. Batter was outfitted in a freshly laundered referee's shirt, unlike the denim work shirt he wore to the gym. The black and white stripes that draped the curve of his gut were trapped in a pair of black Bermuda shorts that went down to his knees but didn't touch them. A pair of white knee-high socks completed his outfit. But, it was his feet that got my attention. They were big like mine and clad in a pair of groovy-red gym shoes. I'd seen nothing that could rival them.

"Greetings. Come on in, Dunker. Glad you brought Dad along. How can I help you today?"

"I need a pair of shoes. The ones you've got on are talking to me. Never seen anything like them before."

"Picked them up years ago when I played ball overseas. Came across them in a small German shop. I wanted a spare pair, but could never find them."

"In that case, I'll try a pair of black basketball shoes that I can go to the prom in."

My eyes shifted from Mr. Batter's scarlet shoes to his wavy slicked-back hair.

"Have a seat over there. Be right back."

Mr. Batter didn't attempt to measure my feet. He knew how to deal with big feet. He had them, and he had fitted the feet of nearly all the teams in town.

When he swaggered back into the showroom, he was balancing six oversized shoeboxes on his hip. He pulled over a footstool with a 30° slant, extending from the front of the seat cushion to the floor. After stacking the boxes at his side, he sat and studied my feet for a moment.

"Put your foot here," he finally said.

Mr. Batter helped me to get the old shoes off and the new ones on.

"Stand up. Walk around some. See how they feel."

My feet were steady and moved with bouncy ease. I went up on my toes, threw a few air hoops, and pivoted from left to right in tight circles.

"These are talking to me, Dad. I'm digging the silver basketball patches over the ankles. I can get my groove on in these."

Nothing more needed to be said about the shoes.

"We'll take them," Dad said.

After he paid Mr. Batter for the shoes, I plucked the box off of the counter and followed Dad out the door. We went back up the street with our usual stride. Dad wasn't as tall as me, but he kept up. When we got to the car, I tossed the shoebox onto the rumble seat and checked my watch.

"We still got time on the clock, Dad. What do we do now?"

"Let's go next door and get a late breakfast."

Kiddy's Cafe was full of early shoppers. It seemed the whole town was abuzz. We waited for seats at the lunch counter where we eventually ate a pancake-bacon-and-egg meal that we rinsed down with goblets of cold milk. When done, we left without a fuss.

DUNKER

Dad and I stood at the curb. We laughed about the girl who served us and how her boobs nearly popped out of her too-tight top onto our pancakes. Dad slapped me on the back with a firm, fatherly hand that felt good.

Back at Big Blue, I made my customary entrance. Hunkering down behind the wheel. Being prom-ready made the drive home a dream. When I pulled into the driveway, Big Blue took a big dip in the curb well. He hardly bounced.

"Sure glad I put new shock absorbers in him. Now, he gives the perfect pitch on a dip."

Dad smiled and said, "It was a nice ride, son."

I let Big Blue roll into the garage, next to Dad's truck, just in case something fell from the sky. My mind kept going back to when Blue was only a chassis and four whitewall tires, brighter than brand-new notebook paper. Blue and Mariah always–I don't know how to put it into classroom English–snatch me around inside my skin.

I got the shoebox from the rumble seat, closed the compartment, and moved toward the house with my eyes on Mom's sweet peas. Paco was at the screen door whining for me to open it.

"Shush, boy," I said.

I inched the door toward me. Paco wagged his cropped tail and jumped at my knees.

"Down boy, not now."

"That you, Dunker?"

Mom's voice floated from the family room, along with the lemon-scented furniture polish to the kitchen, where it contaminated the air.

"Yeah, Mom. It's me."

"Any luck, dear?"

Mom rushed toward me, shrinking the much-needed gap between us.

"I'm ready, Mom," I said and stepped back with a chokehold on the shoebox.

I glanced at Dad sitting at the kitchen table in a less-than-relaxed posture.

"Why don't you take your shoes upstairs? Put them with your tuxedo. We'll surprise Mom later."

Dad stood up and laid the crumpled bit of pink notepaper on the kitchen table. "We're ready for the prom. It can't come soon enough," he told Mom.

He kissed her on the cheek and took refuge in his recliner. Her lips parted ready to speak. She turned to me, but I was charging up the stairs to dodge the questions that might come my way.

I checked on the tuxedo to make sure it was still on the back of the door. I dumped my new shoes on the bed, plucked out toe stuffings, and fired them off to the wastepaper basket.

"Two points."

The extra pair of silver laces in the bottom of the box shoelaces brought a grin to my cheeks. I removed the black laces and maneuvered the tips of silver ones through the eyelets.

I set the basketball shoes side-by-side on the floor, lined up the tuxedo studs on the dresser, and paired the cufflinks with them. Don't know why, just seemed the right thing to do at the time. When my head came up, I caught a glimpse of myself in the mirror. My eye was much better but still had significant bruising around the socket. I snatched socks out of the drawer and tossed a few hoops with them before I changed into a pair of green khaki shorts.

I spent the rest of the day reviewing my Physics notes, writing papers, and reading assignments. I worked through lunch to make sure no tasks were neglected. Finals were coming up and I didn't want a mishap or calamity with Mr. Drew.

The clock's ticktock gave a four o'clock notice that made me glance up. I jumped to my feet to hurry outside. I sat on the back stoop to sort my thoughts.

That's when *Mariah offered her hand for me to take. I did. We danced and we hugged.* I was at the edge of the step about to kiss her when Dad's voice called from the kitchen.

"Come on in. It's time for dinner.

"Where's Toby?" I asked.

"He's still out with Grandma. They're visiting church friends. It's just you and me."

"That's the way I like it."

Dad laughed and kept his, otherwise, possible comments to himself. I sat at the kitchen table with a plate of food my stomach wasn't in the mood to consume. The sweet potatoes, ham, collard greens, and hot water cornbread were too much for me. I ate a bit of meat and swallowed a couple of spoons of vegetables I swished the inside of my mouth with the sweetened, iced tea flavored with lemon slices.

"That's it. I'm done for right now."

"Good enough. Have you washed Blue and cleaned him out?"

"Not yet."

"I wouldn't wait much longer, son."

I got in the car and put my right arm over the back of the seat next to me. When I turned my head to look out the rear window, it was evident that Toby had been playing in Blue. Gum wrappers, half-eaten candy bars, a water gun, baseball shoes, and his muddy football, trashed Big Blue. I thought I was keeping an eye on Toby. I was puzzled when he could have done this. I gritted my teeth with a strong desire to squeeze his neck instead of Blue's steering wheel.

After I backed Blue out of the garage, I raked the trash out of the car and piled it on the driveway 'til I could bag it. I dragged the hose toward Blue and turned the nozzle until the force of the water was equal to my anger. It flipped from my hold and spiraled out of control. I chased the hose. It snaked wildly through Mom's flowers, scattered the trash, and rained down on Big Blue. My hands caught it and choked off the water source.

"Oh! No! This can't be happening to me. Not now. Not at this moment."

"Dunker! You okay, son?"

"It's not good, Dad."

Dad followed the trail of the rubbish until he got to my pointing finger which noted the water standing in Blue.

"You got yourself a big mess there. Get some towels out of the garage and keep tabs on your time."

Dad shook his head and went back inside, abandoning me on my prom night just when I needed him most. I'll never be ready on time.

When I reached for the drying rags, Paco clinched his teeth onto a bunch of the chamois and raced down the street. I was right behind him when one dropped just in time to get caught on my big toe and flipped me.

DUNKER

"Come back here! You sorry mutt."

Not wasting time, I was back on my feet and in pursuit of him.

"You crazy dog, you're about to become enemy number one."

Paco dropped the rags out of fear that I was going to kill him. He was right. I collected the rest from the neighbors' yards and went back to the house.

My day wasn't going well. Toby junked the car. The hose scattered the trash and flooded Big Blue. All this when I had no time to spare.

I kicked the rubbish back into a heap and mopped the water out of Blue. Good thing Granddaddy had put a leather split-back bench in Blue when he did. I wiped it down. My luck, the rumble seat was closed and didn't get wet, or I'd been in double trouble.

I washed and polished the rod 'til it had a perfect shine on its rear end. My eyes scanned it bumper to bumper. It was ready, but the floor was still damp. I left the doors open to create a stronger airflow. I got Dad's duck-taped fan out of the garage loft and plugged it into an extension cord. I aimed the fan toward the front floor of the rod. I left it blowing while I went to shower and dress. I threw a small clean towel on the seat that I had found in the garage.

"When did you get home?

I didn't know how long Toby had been sitting on the back step spying on me, but I was pissed when I realized he was there.

"A while ago," he said.

"We need to talk."

"Go near Blue and you'll be history."

"Your old car don't mean nothing to me."

I got so far into Toby's face, we could've swapped boogers. With my arm stretched behind me and my finger aimed at the rubbish, I said, enunciating each word, "You clean that mess up. It belongs to you."

"I didn't do that."

"It wouldn't be there if it weren't for you. And better not be there when I get back."

"Dunker, where are you?" Mom called.

"Out here."

"It's time, son. Ya gonna be late if you don't

get dressed."

I looked back at Toby. I tightened my lips, pulled my eyebrows together, and upped my fist at him.

"Back to you," Toby said and shoved out his tongue.

"If you want that, you'd better put it back in your head."

"Dunker!"

"I'm right here, Mom. Don't worry. I'll be ready in a jiffy." I kissed her on the cheek. " I'm on my way to the shower. I'll throw on a little aftershave when I'm done."

Beneath a blast of warm water beat down on me as I lathered up. After my twisted gut untangled itself, I scrubbed until I was new-jersey clean. I didn't even want a hint of dirt underneath my fingernails.

After bathing, I wrapped a fresh towel around my waist and stood in front of the mirror. I pumped up my arm muscles, splashed Dad's aftershave lotion on my cheeks, and rolled a deodorant ball around in my armpits. I slipped into my underwear, hoping they didn't itch, new ones do sometimes. I pulled my shoulders back, jiggled my legs, and arched my spine. The boxer shorts passed the itch test.

I went back to the yard, in my bare feet, to check on Big Blue. For once, Toby took me seriously. The driveway was clean and he was not in sight. It was about time something went my way. Blue was dry. I turned off the fan and put it away. I put up the top before backing him out of the driveway. I parked him in front of the house and ran back inside, not wanting the neighbor to see me in my skivvies. It didn't matter to me, but it would have bothered Mom . . . and Grandma, too.

In my room, I flopped on the bed awed at the length of my new socks as I broke the tacky paper band that held them together. I dried between my toes again just to be sure. Coach Ben told us "Keep it dry between the toes if you don't want athlete's feet." I pulled socks on over my big *dogs* and up over my calves. Next, I attached the suspenders to the tuxedo pants and stepped into them. I was fighting the buttons on the tuxedo shirt when Dad knocked on the door.

"How's it going, son?"

"My fingers are so clumsy, I can't get these darn things through the blasted holes."

Dad took over. He pushed the studs through the eyelets with ease. I tucked my shirt in the trousers. My thumbs caught hold of the suspenders and tugged them up and over my shoulders. I let them go with a mighty snap and finished zipping up my slacks. Dad helped clip my tie and cummerbund in place.

While shoving my feet into my brand new sneakers, I let Dad know in a thank you voice, "These shoes we bought look good. And, they're sure enough high steppers. What do you think, Dad?"

After studying my face, he gave me a hasty bear hug that was tighter than usual. Holding me at arm's length, he said, "You're doing okay, son. Finish up and hurry down. Mom, Toby, and Grandma want to look you over," he said with a soft grin.

When Dad shut the bedroom door, the tuxedo coat slammed against it. I donned the coat, adjusted the hanky into the breast pocket, and gave it a pat.

Judith C. Owens-Lalude

Poised, I raised my elbow for Mariah to take hold of my arm. She did. With her arm around me I...

I was about to lead her into a dance formation, but couldn't sense the weight of her hand on my arm. I took off the jacket, stuffed a house slipper into the sleeve, and rammed my arm back into it. The sour foot odor wagered an attack on me. I shook the shoe from the sleeve. It made a loud crackling sound when it smacked against the Venetian blinds and crash-landed into my gym bag.

I lifted my upper body to re-aline the jacket sleeve. The guy in the looking glass could have been a banker, a judge, or maybe the Rev. Glorious. I did a repeat head-to-toe check in the door mirror to ensure nothing was hanging off of me that wasn't supposed to be. My armpits sweated and I hadn't even left the house. Good thing I only had to do this once in my lifetime; too much of it could kill a beastly man.

Dad never had these problems. He was always smooth with Mom. He'd hug her, pat her on her rear, and give her a peck on the cheek when she least expected it. She'd jump, blush, and giggle. Mom would glance from the corner of her eye at Toby and me. We'd laugh and pretend we hadn't seen a thing.

I wondered if Mariah's gonna let me kiss her tonight. The pace of my heartbeat picked up when I moved toward the bedroom door. Before exiting, I looked up at the wall calendar. The days leading up to the prom were X'ed out. Prom day was boxed with red ink. I squeezed the cold, hard, doorknob; gulped, and held onto it. When I peered back over my shoulder, *Mariah winked at me.* Smiling, I pulled the door open, ready to conquer the evening.

An oversized step put me in the middle of the hallway. I felt debonair. No one could tell me that I wasn't *Mr. It*. I headed down the steps to present myself. My heart hammered against my chest wall, the same as it did whenever Dr. Harper raised one of those hypodermic needles to shoot me in the butt. Some things you never get used to. Mariah was added to that list.

Mom, Dad, Toby, and Grandma rushed me when I came off the last step. I had to check myself. For a split second, I thought I was in a playoff game being mobbed by teammates and fans. A second glance validated that it was only my family members.

Wow! Can I shake your hand, Mr. Womack?"

Toby moved toward me with a suspicious grin on his face. I took his scrawny hand and gave it a solid pumping; Mom gave me her prime cautionary stare. I dropped his hand. I didn't want trouble from Mom at this moment.

"Dunker, you look handsome enough to dance with," Mom said as she Box Stepped into my space. Grabbing my hand, she started doing one of those outdated turns. I just stood there and let her hold my hand. She swung herself around while Grandma grinned at us and Dad had a good laugh. Mom abruptly stopped spinning. She braced her hands on her hips like she'd been doing a lot lately. At first, she didn't budge. Then, her mouth moved to say, "Mariah's surely going to be pleased with what she sees tonight."

"Oh, boy! You look damn good."

"Thanks, Grandma."

I hated it when Grandma drew her words out

long as the sweet taffy she pulled arms-length every Christmas Eve.

Grandma lifted her chest and layered her arm across it, making sure her rosary dangled from beneath them. She drew her chin back and heaved big. Grandma did that whenever she was proud of something. But today the look of her pull-tight cheeks spelled concern.

I told Grandma, "You can stop choking that rosary. You're about to crack the beads."

She adjusted it so that I had a better view of the crucifix.

"It's only a prom, Grandma. I can assure you, I won't be dancing with the devil."

"Watch your sass," she said.

"Hold on, there," Mom said. She dashed to the kitchen and back. "You almost forgot these."

I took the flowers, tossed my keys up, and grabbed them in mid-air. I kissed Mom goodbye and said, "See you later," to everyone else.

Doubling back on Toby, I said, "Stay out of my room or I'll plant your face on the back of your head."

"Watch your mouth," Grandma said.

I was at the door ready to leave, but I didn't recognize the person I saw in the glass of the storm door until Mom planted a big one on the side of my face, close to my ear where Mariah anoints me with her affectionate pecks. When Dad opened the front door with the ease of a well-trained butler, the heat of the day smacked at me. I was glad the humidity had taken a break. Now, I could breathe without being drenched in sweat.

"Hey, man. You cool?" Toby hollered.

I jumped the steps and dance-walked on the bricks' zigzag path to the car. I saw myself in Big Blue's shine as I moved near him. The likeness of my blotted body, which swayed back and forth across the cobalt-blue paint looked like a brown-toned, beer-bellied Santa Claus.

I jumped into King Womack's seat, placed the corsage next to me, and turned the key. The motor gunned. Big Blue rocked, coughed, and kicked out a wisp of smoke that wasn't much of anything because the dipstick indicator had shown clean oil. I honked

DUNKER

the horn several times before Blue and I were off–slow and steady–not too fast. I wanted to give the neighbors a chance to see how a tuxedo-clad dude operated a top-notch rod.

When I peeped in the rearview mirror, Mom, Dad, Toby, and Grandma were framed by Blue's oval-shaped rear window. They waited for me to fade out of sight. Grandma's fisted prayer beads squirted sparks.

I laughed and Big Blue grunted. We rounded the corner and disappeared from their sight. I laid my arm on the back of the empty seat next to me to practice hugging Mariah's shoulders. Will she let me kiss her tonight? She always did in my dreams.

10

Timeout
Delilah

After I spent time making kits for Mariah's stupid hair, I rolled it. Although she was sleeping now, her voice chirped in my ear, "Delilah, do this. Delilah, do that."

Fed up, I was glad she was in bed and not up and calling my name. She's been a pain in my backside ever since the day Dunker asked her to go to the prom with him.

Before I got in my bed, I moved nearer to Mariah's to peek at her. Yep. She was a funny sight propped up on those bed pillows with her head lopsided and her limbs dangling over the mattress. She was the perfect picture for the cover of a horror magazine. The caption would read *Spooky Witch on Puffed Up Bed Pillows*.

When the sun filtered through the blinds the next morning, I threw off my covers. Taking my time, I tiptoed toward Mariah's bed. She mirrored a wannabe witch with tear-smeared eyeliner and a silly grin. I hee-hawed so hard, I thought I was gonna wet my pajama pants. I had to squeeze my thighs together and duck-walk to the toilet. I rocked on the potty. Laughing so hard, I 'bout fell off of the seat.

When I returned to Mariah's throne, she was still snoozing. Tuckered out from her craziness, I guessed. Studying her face made me remember Mama's sewing box stuffed with Beek's Cockatiel feathers that she saved for our school projects. A few of them would give Mariah the spark needed for her pre-prom prep.

I brushed back the rowdy plaits that tickled my face and eased across the room. I rushed down the rear stairs to the laundry room quietly because Frisk was outside barking at Miss Donell, the neighbor who lived across the street from us. I pulled Mom's sewing box from underneath the counter and yanked off the rough cord that held it together.

Bang!

The box exploded, Beek screeched, and his gray and yellow feathers spiked. He raced back and forth across the bar hooked front-to-back in his cage, bumping the bell each time he ducked beneath it.

"Hush! Beek. Settle down."

"Who's there? Delilah! That you?"

"Yeah."

"Everything okay?"

"Yeah, Mama. I dropped something."

With the tip of Mama's foot-long knitting needle, I sorted through the scattered whatnots to tease out the feathers. Afterward, I snatched the dustpan from the closet, scooped the needles and notions back into the sewing box, and knotted the cord around it. I didn't have time to make one of Mama's fancy bows. Pressing the feathers against my chest, I stepped easy going back up to the stairs.

DUNKER

Once in the bedroom, I crawled toward Mariah's bed. I raised my head just enough to see her face. She was still dreaming. I stuck a feather, one in each paper kit. The sun, seeping between the blinds, caused them to glisten. Mariah resembled Beek sunbathing on a bad feather day.

I tightened my jaw muscles to not laugh out loud. I rolled over on my back and kicked my bare feet up. Back on my knees, I sat up to glance at Mariah one more time.

I raced out of the room, and back down the stairs. Flopped on the bottom step, I exploded with tear-gushing laughter until my sides ached. It was Mariah's bed squeak that froze me and stopped my heart. Her basketball heels thumped the floor as she walked across the room. Drawers opened and shut with a thud. Nothing to be concerned about. SILENCE. I gasped. I stared wide-eyed into the open space. I didn't blink. The bedroom door opened. It closed. I held my breath.

"Ahaaaaa! You. You. You beady-eyed rat!"

Mariah's feet pounded the floor. She was

coming after me. I got off the step and rushed to the kitchen. Mama was peeling potatoes for breakfast. I stood pancake close to her.

"Mama! Come! Come now!" Mariah hollered.

"What have you done, Delilah?"

"Nothing, Mama."

I shrugged my shoulders and raised my chin so Mama could see I was sincere.

"Mariah, are you okay?"

"No, I'm not okay! Mama, come! Pleeeeease, Mama!"

Crack.

The hairbrush smashed against the vanity. Mama dropped the vegetable peeler. She hastened up the steps two at a time. I followed at a safe distance but didn't go into the bedroom. Mariah was crying and pulling things out of the drawers.

"Where are the scissors?" Mariah cried.

I rolled my eyes. Does she really think those feathers grew out of her head and need to be trimmed? Mama sucked in her lips to not laugh.

"Pluck the feathers out, dear. You'll be okay."

DUNKER

Chuckles pushed against Mama's lips. She coiled her fingers into a fist beneath her nose to stop them from seeping out.

"That's what you always say. Mama! Don't you laugh!"

Mariah opened and slammed the vanity drawers shut. She knocked over her colognes and trophies. Boy-oh-boy, Mariah's already ugly. Now she's mad and I'm in trouble.

I hurried back down to the kitchen to peel the rest of Mama's potatoes. I glanced out of the window above the sink. Daddy was putting back the tulip bulbs that Frisk had dug up to get attention. After he got it, he sneaked back into the house where he curled up in the corner behind Beek's cage–as if a bird could save him from the scolding he was sure to get from Mama.

Footsteps chased Mama's flip-flops down the steps to the kitchen. My heart fluttered. The potato I gripped kept slipping out of my hands. Mariah was screaming, letting Mama know, in harsh terms, how much she hated me and wanted to kill me.

"Mariah, you're gonna knock me down if you don't get off my heels."

Mariah did a mean barefoot tap dance across the kitchen floor. I didn't look her way, but I sensed trouble coming and peeled faster and faster. My hands didn't seem to belong to me anymore.

"Ouch!"

A sting radiated from my nape.

"Help! Help! That hurts!"

The potato peeler flew up and over my head. It dropped to the floor. The next thing I knew, I was kissing linoleum not far from it.

Frisk wagged his tail, yapped at me, and nipped at my nose. He ran in circles wanting to play when there was no playing going on. Mariah yanked my braids and pounced up and down on my back. I think, in her mind, I was a thoroughbred horse that she was riding to the finish post on Derby Day.

"Help! She's killing me. Get her off of me."

Mama's battle arms stretched out. She was about to grab Mariah when Daddy's voice surged from the screened door.

"Stop that nonsense. Immediately!"

The backdoor slammed shut behind him. Frisk raced back to his hiding place beneath the bird's cage. Beek frantically flapped his protest wings. More plumage rained down on the floor.

"Stop it!" Dad said.

Beek mimicked Dad, "Stop it! Stop-it!"

His feathers spiked as he chirped and tracked to and fro across the rod in his cage.

I bucked Mariah as hard as I could. Finally, she flipped over and landed on her back, face up. She cried, kicked, pouted, and pounded her fist. Paper-bag kits crisscrossed the linoleum squares. They were runaway mice with tail feathers. Mama was still braced against the sink with a foothold on her stomach and an arm over her brow. I inched across the floor on all fours to escape the commotion.

"Enough's enough!" Daddy said.

Beek flinched. His bell rang.

I was lifted up by the seat of my pajama pants. Daddy stood me on my feet. With his toughest stare, he said "Small Stuff." That's what Daddy calls me.

"You've just earned a big timeout. Take a book with you. You'll be in that corner for a while."

Daddy stuck his pointer finger right beneath my nose.

"Listen, Daddy. I can explain the whole thing."

"Small Stuff, you had better move it, or you will be in that corner 'til I retire. Look at me. I'm a mighty young man."

"Yeah, 'cause everybody's bent out of shape just because of Mariah and that stupid prom. I can't believe it. All those tears over a few feathers. I shouldn't be in timeout. She should. I tried to explain to you that Mariah pulled my braids. She hit me in the head and jumped on my back while I was trying to help peel potatoes. Mama even tried to get Mariah off me."

Daddy just looked at me. He kept pointing as if I wasn't saying a word.

"Mariah doesn't care about me. She wants to hurt me. Real bad, too."

I lowered my eyelids and turned my face so Daddy could see my hurt expression. Instead, he just kept pointing at the ugly chair. That was the end of our conversation. Frisk followed me to the corner.

"Com'mer, Frisk. Com'mer, Frisk."

"Shut up, you silly copycat cockatiel."

Beek bowed his head, so I could scratch the back of his neck.

"I'm not in the mood for you."

Beek puffed up his feathers and pulled his head down into his fluff, stewing I guess.

I settled myself in the ugly chair. Frisk, the one friend I could always count on, leaped into my lap. He rested his head on the fold of my arm. I stroked his head and braided the long hairs that hung from his ears. I wanted to put ribbons in his hair, but I knew I couldn't get out of the chair until things cooled off. Frisk and I buddied together while we waited for Daddy to realize that I hadn't done anything wrong.

11

The Dance Lesson
Delilah

Mariah finally got herself together, somewhat, and Daddy finally excused me from the corner. Down on my hands and knees, I helped to roll up the carpet in the living room. The teach-Mariah-how-to-dance hour had arrived at our house.

"Let me show you the latest moves. Do as I do," I said to Mariah.

I snapped my fingers, shook my hips, and tapped my foot to a 4/4 beat.

"Let's go. Move it!" I sang.

I slid, I hopped, I turned, I swayed my hips, and rocked them, too. I was grooving. Mariah bumped me, knocked me, and stepped on my toes. Never once

DUNKER

did she step to the beat of the music.

"Let me try, Small Stuff," Daddy said.

"Okay. I'll start the music."

I shrugged my shoulder, put on a 45 record, and sat on the arm of the wingback chair. I watched Daddy. He was tall and good-looking. His skin was smooth and dark. It matched Grandma's and mine. I can tell you, Daddy was the most handsome boy in our English class, Mom always said.

Daddy shook his legs and arms. He did a few deep knee bends. When he stood up straight, his nose was over his shoulder. He could have been a cocoa-brown ballroom dancer. He resembled the ones in the magazines, except they were always white.

Daddy took a steadying breath. He held Mariah's hand, put his long arm around her waist, and pulled her close. Closer than I'd want to be to her.

"Follow me, baby. Hold on to Daddy. We're going to show them how it's done."

"I'm ready, Daddy," Mariah said.

At the just-right beat of the music, Daddy lead

Mariah into a fast dance. He held her hand up for the next move. Mariah moved in and wasted no time taking the shine off the toes of his shoes. Mama hurried to his rescue. She tapped Daddy's shoulder and cut in to keep things from getting too grim.

"Let me try, dear."

"Go ahead, honey. I don't think I'm up to this."

Daddy's smile faded as he backed away. He rested himself on the sofa arm while Mama took over. She had Mariah spinning in circles.

"Hum. Not bad, but she still can't dance," I said to Daddy in secret.

"Hush, Small Stuff, or you'll be back in that corner waiting for my hair to gray."

Mama turned Mariah again and again. Mariah looked almost as good as a real dancer. It was Daddy that I felt sorry for. He was the coolest dancer I knew. He didn't deserve to be battered by Mariah. I had watched him and Mama on evenings when they thought I was in bed.

DUNKER

Daddy would put his arm around Mama's waist. She'd position hers across the back of his neck and rest her head on his chest. Daddy'd stare down on Mama's face. They'd sway for the music to start. He kissed her on the brow before spinning her around. Mama's skirt wings would grab hold of his thighs as they'd glide across the floor where the carpet used to be.

Daddy stood up to reclaim the floor. He sucked in his gut, adjusted his belt, and shook his legs. "Let's try a group dance. Push the sofa further back. Make more room. Spin the 45, Small Stuff."

I lowered the needle. When it touched the record, I took my place next to Mariah, whose foot tapped and hips shifted, as the room filled with make-you-wanna-dance music.

"Cute. Cute. Cute," I said.

"You wanna keep living?" Mariah asked.

"Let's straighten this line," Daddy said.

He snapped his fingers. "1, 2, hit it." We followed his cues. "Right, 2, 3. Left, 2, 3. Back, 2, 3. Dip it. Shake it. Push it. Hop. Hop. Hop."

Judith C. Owens-Lalude

I snapped my fingers, dipped my shoulders, and shook my hips. Mariah's moves were frightful. She resembled a waddling duck chewing gum. She never once hit a beat on time. I had to drop back to keep her off me. That left her bumping Daddy and Mama, too.

"Give it up, Mariah," I said.

"Watch your mouth, Delilah," Mama warned. "You're doing fine, dear," she said to Mariah.

"Let's give it a break," Daddy said.

Just as well. It would have taken Mariah the rest of her life learning the step-hop-step move. That is if she lived to be three hundred and three. The girl's got big feet. Both of them are lefts. Plus, she's always grumpy and has a bad attitude about everything, but Mama and Daddy never noticed. They actually seemed to like her.

"Let's put the furniture back in its place," Daddy said, as the two of us unrolled the carpet.

If the furniture could tell the story about the dance lesson, they'd spin on their gliders, laughing and hooting. I crossed my fingers and hoped that Mariah would do okay at the prom if she didn't break a leg.

12

Pretty in Pink
Delilah

The dance lesson was over. Mariah climbed the steps to what she knew was going to be the greatest day of her life. The first thing she did was gather her new underwear. The bra, panties, and garter belt were placed in body part order with the stockings dangling over the edge of the bed. The slip layered over them topped off the display. Mariah placed the prom shoes underneath the droopy stocking toes. She took a step back to give her arrangement an approving eye.

"What'cha staring at? Didn't Mama tell you to stay away from me? Delilah, you better scat, or I'll fry your you-know-what."

I shrugged my shoulders, backed out of the

room, and crouched on the step near the top of the rear stairway. Mariah skipped out of the bedroom to the bathroom with her new underwear balanced on her outstretched arms, palms up. She reminded me of Mr. Bell the blind man on the corner, the day that she almost flattened him coming out of the shoe shop.

Mariah must have knocked the bathroom door shut with her hip or foot. Her feet whisked back and forth kicking slits of light from beneath the door. The medicine cabinet door cranked. *Wham.* It slammed shut.

Water collected in the sink. *Splash.* Quiet. The stopper chain rattled. *Pop. Slurp.* The sucking and swishing water noises were replaced with a tooth-brushing sound that was followed by gargling, spitting, and light kicking.

The cuckoo clock struck three times a while ago. A hushed moment stretched itself out. The shower curtain crunched. Its rings scratched along the metal shower rod like fingernails on a chalkboard. Water pipes clanked. The shower water gushed a fussy spray.

DUNKER

Oh! No! Mariah is belting out the school song. That's not good. She should give it up and come on out of the bathroom. She can't dance and she can't sing either.

Bop. The soap dropped. *Shoosh.* It skidded.
Bop. Shoosh. Bop.

Guess she can't hold onto the soap. Silence. Shower spray. Nothing. I stretched my neck. I waited, still nothing. Waited more.

"Mariah, you okay? It's after four o'clock," I said, just loud enough for her to hear.

"What's it to ya?"

The shower handle clanked when Mariah turned the water off. The curtain rings that dragged against the metal bar, puckered my skin like a country-plucked chicken. The towel rack rattled. Daddy keeps saying he's going to fix those loose screws. Now he's got an extra one to tighten.

"Hehehe!"

Shoo. Shum.

The toilet flushed.

I continued waiting with my head resting on

my forearms. There was a mix of fragrances from the lotion, cologne, and body powder that slithered from beneath the bathroom door. They made me sneeze. I dabbed at my nose with the ruffle of my red and yellow plaid halter top. After waiting an additional hour, the cuckoo clock cooed the five o'clock warning. The bathroom doorknob rattled as it was turned.

I ducked down, pulling myself small. Mariah emerged from her sanctuary. Her hair kits were gone. The curls on her head stood unsupported and at attention. She was bedecked in her new dusty pink, satiny, lacy, underwear, pretty enough to wear without a dress, but something was missing. Mariah's bare feet moved her too fast for me to be sure.

The prom dress was still in the box held closed with the pink ribbon. She finger-tipped the bow in a way that reminded me of the day she stroked a baby bird blown out of its nest. She wouldn't let anyone near it.

Now, Mariah didn't want anyone to touch her stupid dress, not even Mama, who wanted to give it a light pressing.

DUNKER

While sitting on the vanity stool, Mariah lifted one of the limp stockings. She pulled it on over her long-as-finger toes and up her flag-pole leg to fasten it to the garter belt. She did the same with the stocking's mate. She stretched her legs to admire them.

"Stay out of Mariah's way," Mama said when she passed me on the steps, where I spied on Mariah. It's my room, too, but it didn't seem to belong to me anymore.

Mama placed a small beaded handbag, not much larger than my open palms, butted together, and a pair of opera gloves on the vanity. She clasped her hands, hastened out of the room, and down the hallway, back to her bedroom. Drawers opened and closed. Small boxes bumped each other, trinkets clacked, and tissue paper crunched. Mama was on a scavenger hunt.

Mariah slid her feet into the prom shoes. With her knees together, she swayed them back and forth. *Miss Cutie Pie* on a throne, but not on a Halloween one. With her raccoon nose pointed upward and her knees still together, she twisted herself from side to side. She kicked her heels up, again and again, as if she were a New York Rockettes until she fell off her vanity-stool throne. I rolled my eyes and plugged my mouth with my fist as Mama did her's when she answered Mariah's call about the feathers stuck in her paper kits. I didn't want the laughter to escape and reveal my location. There was no need to get into any more trouble with Mama. She'd send me over to help Mrs. Donell to do whatever chores the two of them might come up with. I didn't need to be removing caterpillars from the fence today. I did that not long ago after I frizzed Mariah's hair with the eggbeater. Mama's mind can be creative at times and this might be one of them.

    Mariah unscrambled herself and got back on her feet. She checked her stockings for runs and sat back down on her throne with slumped shoulders that didn't seem so royal anymore.

    Mama was back. She had crying eyes and looked almost sickly. Guess she didn't find what she was looking for. She picked up the beaded bag from the dressing table. Coins jingled inside it when she put it back down. Mama turned and lifted up the gown box, but set it back down. She must be confused about something.

Mariah touched the satin bow on the dress box. When she caught hold of the ribbon, her chest heaved. With more grace than I'd ever seen, she pulled it toward her heart until the smooth, pink knot popped apart. In the slightest motion, Mariah lifted the lid. She *oooed*. Mama *ahhhed*. They had the sound of two old grandmas eyeing a brand-new baby. That was my cue to get lost. I joined Daddy downstairs.

"What's up, Small Stuff?"

"Not much. Mama's helping Mariah to get dressed."

Daddy must have heard me coming. He was standing at the bottom of the front stairs. For a minute, he resembled a statue cut from stone. His eyes were still and blank. His gaze was fixed as if he saw someone who wasn't there. He didn't go up to our bedroom anymore. He told us "You girls are too big for me to visit."

"Come on, Daddy. She'll be down soon."

I took Daddy's hand. It was cold and dry. I led him to the living room. We sat on the sofa. I moved close to him to make small talk, but Daddy didn't respond. I guess his mind was on Mariah. I laid my head against his shoulder. Frisk huddled in between our feet and licked my leg. I wished Mariah was that nice to me. Maybe, I should turn her into a dog.

"Hehehe!"

"What are you laughing about, Small Stuff?"

"Oh . . . nothing. Just thinking."

Daddy wouldn't appreciate my joke.

"I'm going back up to check on Mariah for you." Daddy nodded his head. He didn't smile like he usually does.

At the top of the backstairs, I crawled along the wall. With my index finger, I pushed the door ajar enough to see inside. Mama held a pink cloud above Mariah's head. Mariah stuck her arms through the middle of it so she could push them through the capped sleeves. When she wiggled her hips, chiffon glided down over the crinoline slips fastened at her waist.

"Oh, Mama, it's sooo pretty."

DUNKER

Mama zipped up the back of the fitted bodice. She stood back. With the butt of her hand, she blotted tears that wet her cheeks. Mama rushed from the prom room to her bedroom. Drawers rolled in and out once more. There were crunching, clattering, and bumping sounds. Mama's working herself into a tizzy. Whatever she's looking for, I hope she finds it this time.

Mama eased back into our room. Not wanting to be noticed, she awkwardly rested herself against the wall. Although she still had tears on her cheeks, I think she found what she was looking for. So, I didn't understand all this mush-mush going on. It made me want to gag. Mama and Mariah needed to get on with it. It's only a prom.

Mariah gawked at her gloriousness in the mirror and never knew that Mama had gone and come back. Mariah reached down and pinched the sides of her skirt. Without a thought, she lifted it and turned her body. She was the tiny ballerina in her jewelry box when it was about to stop turning. Her long, pink legs moved with ease. They turned her around, creating a gentle breeze that lifted the chiffon skirt up off of its crinoline

Judith C. Owens-Lalude

support. A soft ring of pink fluff swirled about her tall, slim body.

Mariah captured the skirt's sides and curtsied low, near to the floor as chiffon peaks collared her body. When she gracefully rose to her feet, she saw Mama's withdrawn reflection in the mirror goggling at her.

"I love it, Mama."

Mama hugged Mariah. "You'll be the belle of the ball this year. You're splendid enough to be an African Queen."

Mariah cast her eyes downward. She blushed and giggled quietly. She settled down on her throne. My bedroom was converted into a beauty parlor. Mama brushed Mariah's hair and finger-waved it. She used hairpins and bobbie pins to hold the style in place.

"That's good, Mama."

Mama eased back a few paces. "It's ready for the finishing touches."

Mariah clipped a string of miniature pearls on each side of her head just above her temples. She fastened tiny, pink, silk roses among the curls. She powdered her face, lined her eyes, blushed her cheeks, and colored her lips. Mariah was mesmerized by the vision in the mirror that blossomed with elegance.

"I'm ready, Mama," she said, still not shifting her gaze away from the looking glass.

Mama pulled a thin, delicate, gold chain from her pocket. A single pearl dangled from it. She draped it around Mariah's neck with shaky fingers that could hardly fasten the clasp.

Still fighting tears, Mama said, "You're beautiful, my dear."

"Chin up, Mama. It's only a prom."

Mariah pecked Mama on the cheek to reassure her, but it didn't work. Tears washed over Mama's high cheekbones. One would think she'd be glad someone had enough courage to take Mariah someplace. I wouldn't take her to the church *giveaway*. One of the families might get her, be cursed by the gift, and return Mariah to us.

I've been praying a lot since this prom thing started. First, for Mariah who acted up on the basketball court; Daddy, the lost soul; and now for Mama, whose crying about all those nothings. What next?

"Enough," I said to myself.

I scooted on my belly across the floor, poked my pointer finger underneath the door, and pulled it shut without the slightest bang. I went back down the stairs to sit with Daddy. He was on the couch where I left him. Only now, he was reading the *Holy Bible*. I'm sure he's praying for Dunker, who had to spend his prom night with Mariah.

Frisk had jumped up on the sofa and was snuggled against Daddy, whose hand rested on his back for moral support. I scooped Frisk up, lapped him, and took his place next to Daddy. Frisk had warmed the spot for me.

"Everything okay, Small Stuff?"

"Yeah, Daddy. Mariah's almost ready."

DING-DONG.

"That must be Dunker," I said.

Daddy went to answer the door. I dropped Frisk on the sofa and dashed back up the stairs to tell Mariah that Dunker was at the door. I missed my footing and clipped my nose on the edge of the step.

"Ouch!"

Blood trickled down my upper lip, so, instead, I rushed to the bathroom to splash cold water on my face, pinch my nose, and hold my head back.

"Drat! Pickles!"

I twisted toilet paper to make plugs for my nose. I stuffed a wad into each nostril and hurried back to my post on the top step.

The door to the bedroom, not mine anymore, was opened about three inches. Mama was hugging and kissing all over Mariah. I hoped that Mama's lips didn't blister.

"That must be Dunker. Take your time, dear. Come down when you're ready," Mama said as her eyes critiqued Mariah's hair and gown.

As Mama went out of the door she blew her nose into a tissue and pulled the doorknob behind her. She sleepwalked down the hallway. I pushed the door open just a hair. Mariah was in the center of the room examining what she saw in the mirror. She smiled a smile I'd never seen before. She's a strange one.

Mariah adjusted her skirt and sleeves. She spun around more carefully this time, not wanting to muss up the ruffling on her gown. She stopped suddenly and scooped up the to-your-elbow gloves, beaded bag, and scarf from the dressing table. The prom-goer glided toward the door. With her eyes closed, she reached for the doorknob.

"This is it," she said.

Mariah widened her eyes and blew out the longest breath ever as she pushed the door fully open to step into the hallway. At the top of the front stairs, she fumbled with her handbag as she stuffed her fingers into the gloves and pulled them to her elbows. She fluffed the layers of her skirt before descending the stairs.

With my body against the floor, I belly-slid myself back down the rear steps to take my place at Daddy's side. He was shaking hands with Dunker. Daddy peered over his shoulder at me.

"What happened to you, Small Stuff?"

DUNKER

"Hurt my nose, Daddy." I grinned from behind the tissue that jotted from my nostrils and pointed at Daddy's chin.

"Get some ice for your nose."

"Okay, Daddy."

I didn't move. I put my hands over my nose to hide the wads.

"Have a seat," Mama said to Dunker, as she came down the front steps. Her eyes were red and allergy puffy. "Mariah will be down soon," she said.

Dunker shifted himself but remained standing in his selected spot. He rocked nervously as he swung a corsage box back and forth ball-style. He's gonna have himself a floral milkshake if he keeps that up.

I stepped back for a better look at the *Prom King* that was underneath my roof. Dunker's bony wrists played peek-a-boo at the hems of his tuxedo sleeves. My eyes followed the glossy, satin strip that tracked down the side of his pant legs and slammed to a halt, too far above his ankles. His big *paddle feet* were clad in new, shiny, ink-black gym shoes. Ahhh, those glittering shoelaces. Not to mention the silver basketball patches over the ankles that had a shine that could challenge the yellow glow of the dress Mariah considered buying.

Dunker just isn't the boy I dreamed of going to my prom with. Good thing he was Mariah's date. She got what she deserved, a tall dude in a black minuscule tuxedo, wobbling in fancy oversized *boats*. If God created man in his own image, I wondered what he thought about this guy standing here.

"Oh, dear me," Mama mumbled.

Mariah was finally coming down the stairs. Her eyes twinkled as she placed each foot down on the step as if it might not be there to receive it. She was a gorgeous chestnut brown. Her cheeks were rosy. Her neck and chest glistened under the light of the day. She had the look of a beautiful bride in pink. Better yet, one might say, a pretty brown Cinderella. She was the perfect picture of a *Prom Queen*. She could have just stepped out of one of my storybooks. Mariah was actually beautiful. I didn't think it could be done.

"Wow!" I said.

In my state of disbelief, my hands slid from

my nose to my chin.

"Mama! Look at her. Get that bloody-nosed creature out of here."

And maybe, I'd slam the book shut on her glass slippers.

With his mouth half-opened and eyes squinted, Daddy strained to decipher what he saw. "Is this my little girl? You look . . . You look like a lady. A real pretty . . ."

Daddy tried to say something more, but he was paralyzed. Mama had gone and returned from the kitchen with Dunker's boutonnière. She handed it to Mariah who moved into Dunker's zone, but not as she did on the basketball court when she blocked his shots. She pinned the pink, rose boutonniere to his lapel. It somersaulted with the tail of it pointed upward. Mariah's eyes filled with surprise.

"Humm," she said.

Mama was calm. She removed the boutonnière and handed it back to Mariah.

"Take your time, dear."

I squeezed my gut to keep my snickering under

control. Mariah shot another one of her nasty looks at me. I patted my foot and hoped blood from my nose would fart out the plugs and splatter her gown with red polka dots. That would serve her right. I gave her my I-dare-you-to eye. She knew there was nothing she could do to me gift-wrapped in all that chiffon. I'd have her tied into a fancy pink knot before she could lift her cotton-candy skirt to chase me.

Mariah didn't look into Dunker's face as she successfully pinned her target.

Dunker gasped and stepped back with relief. Purple and green ribbons coiled around his long monkey fingers when he took the flowers, he brought with him, out of their box. He sat the empty container on the edge of the telephone table that Daddy had glued back together.

Shaking like a ninety-year-old man, Dunker reached toward Mariah. He attempted to pin the corsage to her dress, but the flowers catapulted from his grip. Daddy picked them up with a reassuring smile. With a blood-drained face, Dunker backed into the telephone bench, knocking it against the wall.

DUNKER

I put up my hands to help Dunker balance as he recovered his footing.

"Mama! Don't let her touch him. She's a bloody beast."

I rolled my eyes hard as I could. I showed Mariah the back of my head and flipped my braids at her. When my eyes refocused, I noticed the snug bodice that flattened her breasts and her brain. That's it! Her 32 AA padded bra wasn't there. Mariah moved so swiftly when she came out of the bathroom, I didn't see it. But now, I know she's not wearing it. Boy! Oh, boy! Wait 'til Mama figures that out. Mariah is gonna be fried. One thing you don't do at our house is go out with a piece of your underwear missing.

Daddy handed Dunker the flowers. The basketball all-star moved close to the pink gown. Again, his hands were a flock of sparrows splashing in a birdbath. There was no way he'd catch hold of that gown to fasten anything to it. He tried, but the pearl-tipped hatpin had a mind of its own and was airborne. Several spins later, it hit the floor. Dunker became a long and tall stalagmite like the ones I saw in Mammoth

Cave. Dunker didn't even blink. Daddy picked up the pin and gave it to Dunker. Daddy was the pick-it-up guy–first the flower, now the hatpin.

"Try again, son," Daddy said.

Dunker was coming apart right in front of my eyes. Could this possibly be the same guy who shot baskets from mid-court, netted the ball, and had the steadiest hands on the team? I wondered what his teammates would think if they saw him now. I could super-glue him back together and stick his arms on in reverse. That he could shoot balls from the back of his head.

"Hehehe!"

"What are you laughing at?" Mariah growled.

I stuck my fingers in my ears and wagged my tongue, hoping my bloody plugs would fall at her feet. I turned my head and flicked my braids at her again. This time, it was with an I-dare-you-to-come-after-me signal. The plugs popped out, but there was no blood or gush, to my disappointment. I kicked the wads aside.

"Mama, you need to lock that girl up," Mariah mumbled between her gritted teeth.

DUNKER

"All will be fine, dear. Delilah . . ."

I left, but I was back in a flash with fresh toilet paper up my nose. This time, I put my nose up for better viewing. Who was Mariah to tell me to get lost?

"Mama! Look at her. Can't you do something about her? She's grossing out everybody."

Mama gave me the usual cautionary glance. I eased behind Daddy and hugged him.

"Behave, Small Stuff," he said from over his shoulder.

Mama went about the business of helping Dunker poke voodoo pins into Mariah's chest.

"Why don't you place the corsage on her wrist?" Mama said.

Dunker laid the hatpin next to the flower box. He stretched the elastic band on the underside of the corsage, slipped it over Mariah's wiggly hand, and smiled with relief. Mariah's lips went ear-to-ear. She flashed every tooth that God had given her, or maybe it was the devil. Good-golly! That girl's orbiting.

Dunker gave Mama a *Thank-You* glance and took hold of Mariah's arm. In no time, they were out the door. Mama eased forward to go after Mariah, but Daddy held her back.

"She's all grown up now. I've prayed that God will go with her."

Mama turned toward Daddy. She stared point blank, into his eyes. "I put dimes in her purse to call home if she needs to." Mama's face was still flush with concern. Heavy tears pushed at her eyelids.

"Don't be late getting home."

I don't think they heard Daddy's meek voice. Mariah and Dunker were shuffling down the sidewalk toward Big Blue. Mama, Daddy, Frisk, and I stood four abreast on the front porch to monitor the prom couple. Mariah and Dunker didn't even look back to see if we were watching them.

Dunker pulled the car door open for Mariah. She lowered her rear to the seat. Chiffon whooshed up to her prom curls. She pulled her feet underneath the skirt. Pushing downward, she stuffed the fluff beneath the dashboard and held it until Dunker shut the car door. Afterward, she drew a sheer lavender scarf, accented with purple flowers and a scattering of lime-

DUNKER

green leaves, over her new hairdo.

From the driver's side, Dunker slid in next to Mariah. After settling down, Dunker made a few adjustments and gunned the motor. I bet Mariah was tapping the toes of her shoes on the footboard and counting a 4/4 beat to keep time. I wished her luck.

The car took off. Mama's tears did, too. She clutched her chest for the heart attack she wasn't having. I wondered if Dunker would kiss Mariah. No one budged until Big Blue was out of sight. Not even Mrs. Donell, who peeked at the scene through her parted blinds. For some reason, she was never too ill to meddle in our business, at least Mariah's and mine.

13

Dribble and Drive
Delilah

The prom must be over, since Mariah's coming up the stairs, sounding like a swishing bush. She bounded through the door grasping a good-sized trophy.

"What's that you got?" I asked.

"I'll tell you later."

"Tell me everything. Don't leave anything out."

Mariah pushed her gloves down to her wrists and tugged them off, one fingertip at a time.

"Tell me now."

"Unzip me."

After I did, Mariah kicked off her prom shoes and wiggled the digits at the end of her feet.

"That feels good. My toes felt as if they were

crawling over the backs of each other."

Mariah gathered her cotton-candy skirt, pushed it up to her head, and disappears inside the heap of pink. When she reappeared, she clustered it in her arms and pretended to dance with it as if it were a special person. Dunker, of course. I hoped that she didn't step on his toes in her daydream.

Mariah tossed the dress on her bed. She unsnapped the stockings from the garter belt, and rolled them down her legs, over her heels, and off her toes. They were the abandoned pink donuts on the floor.

Mariah slipped into her nightgown. I didn't notice if she wore a bra or not. I wasn't going to ask. She was already acting strange enough and I wanted to hear what else she had to say.

Mariah pounced on her bed and drew her legs up inside her nightgown. She cradled them and rested her chin on the kneecaps. Her face changed, same as it did the days leading up to tonight: at the park with Dunker, in the dress shop, by the magazine rack, in the beauty shop, going out the door to the prom, and now. How many shades of brown can one person turn? Mariah was a chameleon in a nightgown.

"If I tell you something, you can't tell a soul."

Mariah grinned wide. She nervously batted her eyelashes the same as she did on the basketball court with Dunker.

"I won't," I whispered with my most secretive voice.

"Cross your heart and hope to die?"

I drew an enormous make-believe cross over the front of me. With soft, rushed words, I said, "I've crossed my heart."

"Delilah, if you speak a word of what I tell you, I won't ever speak to you again. Not for the rest of my life. My children won't even look at you."

Mariah sat lotus style, with her bed pillows on her knees. She perched her elbows on them and leaned toward me. I kept quiet, not sure if she was going to tell me something or slip into one of her *crazies*.

Looking me directly into my eyes, Mariah said, "Remember when Dunker and I left the house for the prom?"

"Yeah, yeah."

"Well, Dunker took me to the 24-Hour Curb-a-Burger. We ate cheeseburgers and French Fries and sipped on chocolate shakes. He even brought a towel along for my lap."

"Did you eat onions? You usually do."

"Not this time."

"'Cause you wanted Dunker to kiss you. Didn't you?"

"Don't talk, Delilah. Just listen.

"After we left Curb-a-Burger, we drove on to the prom. Dunker parked the car. Again, he opened the door for me. He never opens the doors of his hotrod for anybody. He always jumps over them, getting in and out. This made me think that he actually likes me. Dunker even offered his hand to me. It was warm and sweaty, but I didn't mind. Tonight it felt good. He helped me out of the car just like Daddy does when he takes Mama out."

"Wow!"

"When I tilted my head, I saw Dunker smiling at me. Lord! I thought I was going to die. Dunker's tall, but at that moment, his head seemed to touch the clouds.

Judith C. Owens-Lalude

From underneath all that dress, I swung my legs around to put my feet down on the ground, but I couldn't move. For some reason, the ground didn't seem to be there. My ankles were wobbly, so I repositioned my feet more firmly on the ground and prayed they wouldn't disappoint me. Just at that moment, Dunker raised his elbow. I hooked my arm with his. His muscles rippled beneath my touch. Boy. Oh boy! Dunker is Superman strong."

"Don't go off into one of those imaginary trips. Get on with the story."

"From the parking lot, I stared at the six steps leading up to the gym. They appeared to be thin strips of concrete only suitable for dolls' feet. When we got to the steps, I told myself that I would make it up to the doors."

With the fingers of the hand that clutched my purse and scarf, I lifted the front of my skirt to not step on the hem. Halfway up the stairs, I felt my body falling. I held tighter to Dunker's arm, quivering like a gelatin salad. I thought I was going to faint.

I unfolded my legs and sat on the edge of my

bed, quizzically looking at Mariah.

"You didn't! Did you?"

I held my breath and waited for the answer.

"Relax. I stayed on my feet."

My body fell back into a soft curve as Mariah continued with her evening's details.

"Dunker opened the gym door for us. We eased in and stood beneath an arc of purple and green balloons. A breeze blew my skirt back, creating pink-shinny shimmers. Dunker gazed into my eyes. I thought I was going to fly away. 'You want to sit with the girlfriends or sit with the guys?' he asked. I didn't want to join any gossipy girls talking about boys, clothes, lipstick colors, parties, and movies. Besides, they didn't know a thing about basketball. 'With the team,' I said. I positioned my feet, readying them for the walk across the dance floor. 'You all right?' Dunker asked me. I tried to smile, but I couldn't."

Mariah made a tight-lip grin, bobbed her head, and raised her shoulders.

"After our eyes adjusted to the dark, Dunker led his Queen, that's me, to the tables where the players and their dates sat as if they were at a royal banquet. The guys quickly got to their feet as we approached them. They shook hands with Dunker and barely took note of me. Dunker had told me earlier that Sly was going to bring his sidekicks to the prom, but they walked in with their own dates. One with a cheerleader. The other with a majorette. Both girls were cute."

Mariah closed her eyes and fisted a bunch of her dress. When she opened them she said, I was so nervous that I didn't remember if the guys had said anything to me or not. They sat back down with their dates and Dunker pulled a chair out for me, just like . . . "

"I know. Daddy does for Mama."

"That's right."

"What happened next?"

Mariah rolled her eyes at me. "You're getting too pushy. Just shut up and listen."

Mariah kept chattering. She had a story to tell, more superior than her half-court shots.

"Sly sat across from us. He wore a black Sunday suit. His date was Sara. Good thing she had on high heels. Standing in them, her head was only

DUNKER

elbow-high to Sly's arm.

"When I raised up to smooth my skirt underneath me, Dunker asked me to dance. The shock knocked me off my petticoats. He had to catch me and put me back on my seat. I was so embarrassed that I . . . "

"You didn't cry, did you?"

"No."

"What did Dunker say?"

"He didn't say anything."

"He grabbed my arm and took me straight to the middle of the dance floor. He held my hand and put his arm around my waist. He pulled me close. I put my arm across the back of his shoulder mimicking the dancers around us."

"How close?"

"Close enough I felt his heart beating against my chest. That's when I started to pray for God to please help my feet do the right thing."

You mean, you were chest-to-chest, and no bra, I wanted to say, but Instead, I blurted, "I hope it was a fast dance."

"Shut up, Delilah. No. It wasn't fast. If it was, how could we have been chest-to-chest? The Lord heard my prayers. He kept the music slow to give my feet a chance to adjust to the idea of dancing."

Mariah looked down at her dress. It covered most of her bed.

"Dunker led, I tried to follow, but something went wrong. His feet ended up underneath mine."

"Oh, no! You didn't, Mariah!"

"I did, but my dress was long enough to hide it. Nobody knew but Dunker. He was cool about it. When the music stopped, my legs tried to buckle beneath me. 'Let's get something to drink,' Dunker said, just in time. I clamped onto his arm not sure I'd make it to the drink table. Lucky for me, he led the way. If he hadn't, I'm sure, I'd been a permanent fixture on the dance floor."

"It's a good thing you didn't get that little, light blue, funny looking, shirttail dress. But, go on. Tell me what happened next."

I pulled my legs back up, crossed them, and waited for Mariah's words. She studied the ceiling and thought for an extremely long moment. To not upset her, I pushed my pillow up to my mouth, where Mariah wanted it to stay, if she had the choice to put it there.

"After we got our drinks, we went back to the table. I heard something come through the speakers. I'm not sure what the announcement was about. I was still flustered from the first dance. 'Let's go, Mariah,' Dunker said.

"We put our drinks down and headed back to the dance floor. This time, the music was fast. The beat was powerful and the floor was crowded. Dunker and I danced with my front to his. I counted the way Daddy said I should, 'One, two, three, hit it.' I moved in and out, but my beat was off. On the fourth beat, I clobbered Dunker's toes. I tried to . . ."

"You danced on his feet again. Didn't you?"

Mariah pointed her finger straight at the flesh between my eyes and said, "Focus, Delilah."

"Okay! But, what did Dunker say?"

"He was cool. He led me off the dance floor, out of the gym, and down the hallway. When I saw the sign, GIRLS, the fruit punch I had drank filled my bladder. I told Dunker to wait a moment. I went into the Girls' Room. When I came out, he was leaning against the wall. 'Okay. What's up, Dunker? Is something wrong?' He straightened up and put his hands on my shoulders. 'We need a dance plan,' he said. He grabbed me by the waist, we're gonna be laughed off the floor he told me as he led me down the hallway and around the corner."

"Did you cry?"

"I was too numb to. The whole prom thing was beating up on me, and this dance thing had become a substantial thorn in my drawers."

"Hehehe! What did you say to him? What did you do?"

"Don't you laugh. Just listen. I really don't remember saying anything, but I knew something had to be done. Dunker said that when we got back out on the dance floor, we were going to pretend to play ball. Right there in the hallway, we did a few moves and created cues. We practiced until we had our routines down."

"What about music?"

"No problem. The sound of the band could be heard throughout the building."

"Then, what?"

Mariah put her hand up in a *stop* motion way. "You're trying to shove me through this recall. I need to take my time telling you what happened. Shut up and listen."

Mariah took in a deep breath. When she finally let it out, she continued with her stupid story.

"After we mastered the routine, we went back to the gym and straight to the dance floor. It seemed as if we were alone in the crowd. The music was great. We locked eyes and waited to catch the beat. 'Let it rip,' Dunker said. My hands jotted up. Dunker gave me a double high-five. We bumped hips, two, three, four. We locked hands, two, three, four. We kept a steady beat 'til Dunker gave the next cue. 'Guard me, Mariah,' he said. I spread out my arms."

Mariah flung her limbs over her head and fanned them out as she went on with the story.

"Dunker stooped with his arms stretched out to his sides. He rocked his hips to the beat of the drum.

Judith C. Owens-Lalude

'Switch,' he yelled. His arms went up and mine reached out."

Mariah opened her arms as if to hug her lost-and-found friend.

"I bent my knees and swung my hips to the rhythm of the drums. I swung them good, too!

I was about to open my mouth to say something, but Mariah's rubber-duck smile faded and the dark centers of her eyes let me know I'd better not speak. I swallowed my words.

"'Give me a nice shot,' Dunker yelled. I went up on my toes. I made a *fire-hot* free throw. 'Switch,' he said. He duplicated my move. 'Keep it going, Mariah.' We were electrifying. So much so, that all the dancers moved back and gave us the entire floor. We did our dribbles and drives. I positioned the make-believe ball for a high-arching shot. We turned in circles, just as we did when we each guarded our man in the real games. Dunker made the calls. I created the steps. The prom-goers couldn't wait to return to the dance floor. They grooved to our funky moves. The gym rocked. We didn't sit down after that. I was glad I didn't get that yellow dress that blinded Mama. I wouldn't have been able to shake my *thing* or make those moves."

Mariah and I laughed 'til tears spilled from our eyes.

"See that trophy over there?"

"Un-hun."

"You'll never guess, in the lifetime of a turtle, what it's for."

"Best dressed?"

"No."

"Best couple?"

"No. It's for Best Dancers."

"You're kidding."

I laughed and kicked my legs the same as that tortoise might, if he were on his back.

"How did you manage that?" I asked when I recovered from my hysteria.

"If you stop that crazy laughing, I'll tell you."

"Okay. Okay."

Mariah got up on her knees and sat back on her heels.

Judith C. Owens-Lalude

"Once my jitters were gone, Dunker and I danced every dance. We jumped and jammed. I never stepped on his toes again. Toward the end of the prom, the DJ announced, 'Dance contest. Couples only.' The gym was damp and steamy. The floor was packed with bodies. The judges tapped shoulders and dancers vanished from the floor. Dunker and I smiled because we were still alive. He threw up both hands. I slapped them. After we did a front-to-front and back-to-back, again, and again, the third time we were eye-to-eye. Dunker said, 'Give me a hoop.' I did. 'Double back,' he said. I did a dribble-drive and turned in reverse. When we were side-to-side, Dunker hollered, 'Guard me.' I turned in front of him and cast my arms out. He dropped to a stoop stance. 'Switch,' he said. I bent my knees and swished my hips.

"The judges were still tapping shoulders. Only a few couples remained on the floor. A judge came toward us. We're going to get it, I thought.

"I closed my eyes and bit down on my lip. I can do this, I told myself. 'Double five. Rock-rock.' My voice came up from nowhere. Dunker smiled big.

DUNKER

He gave me the thumbs-up sign. He took my hands and spun me into his chest and out, not once but twice. I threw up my hands. We interlocked fingers. I slid between Dunker's legs and came up with a spring that got an ovation. The judge changed his course to tap a nearby couple. Dunker, still holding my hands, crisscrossed my arms in front of me. He pulled my right hand, spinning me away from him. That's when the music stopped. We were the only couple left on the floor. 'Can this be? Can this really be?' I kept saying. Dunker let go of my hand to receive a trophy. The judge handed a trophy to me. I never heard the announcement. I'm sure something was said. The crowd laughed and cheered."

Mariah stopped talking. She glanced in the mirror and paused. She turned, look at me, and said, "Remember, I told you that I had something to tell you? But, you can't tell a soul."

"Uh-huh."

"I'm in l-o-v-e."

"You! In love? Can't be."

Judith C. Owens-Lalude

I shoved my bedding aside, unfolded my legs, and got in her face.

"Where did you get that idea from?"

"Because, whenever Dunker looked at me, or put his arms around me, my insides trembled, my feet froze, and my legs tried to fold up underneath me. Plus, whenever he kissed me, I wanted him to kiss me again and again. I think. My head was . . ."

"Kiss! Yuck! Did you kiss him back?"

"I don't know. I think so. I'm not sure."

"Think so? Not sure? If a boy kissed me, and I kissed him back, I'd know it."

"Don't you worry. No one will come close to putting their lips on you. And, guess what else? I held on to Dunker's arm most of the night."

"What did he think about that?"

"He never pulled away."

"Okay! Get on with the story, Mariah."

After Mariah rolled her eyes at me, she stretched out on her throne and stared at the ceiling.

"When they played the school song, everyone sang along. We knew that the next song would be, *The*

DUNKER

Dance Is Over. I was happy that Dunker had basketball hands and arms. He draped them over my shoulders. With his trophy pressed against my back, I wrapped both of my arms around him. We danced slowly and sandwich close. When the music stopped, I didn't want the dance to end, but the bright lights came on."

"Good thing you were dancing in the dark all that time. If somebody had seen you and told Mama, you'd be in trouble I wouldn't be able to get you out of."

"Don't talk, Delilah.

"I glanced around me. The gym had the look of carpenter ants marching through a tub of rainbow sherbet. I hadn't noticed the beautiful pastel gowns that the girls wore or the tuxedos that the boys had on. They marched out penguin style in their dark suits."

"Hehehe!" Mariah and I laughed.

When Mariah regained my composure, she continued. "When we approached the table, Sly jumped up. 'Man, you guys were good out there. I was digging your moves,' he said.

"Dunker shook hands with him and they slapped

one another on the back. The other players stacked fists with him while the girls cackled among themselves. I collected my things and put my gloves back on. When Dunker offered his arm, I clasped onto it. We walked across the gym to the open doors. My feet practically danced across the floor. My legs were as steady as goalposts going down the steps," Mariah giggled.

"Yeah, 'cause that trophy was going to your head."

"You'd better get a hold of yourself if you want to hear how things ended."

14

The Overlook
Mariah

Delilah fluffed up her pillow, laid her head down, covered up, and waited. I stared straight ahead. My eyes shifted. My lips started to move but didn't.

I fluffed my dress laying on my bed before telling Delilah that there was no need to lift my skirt going down the steps. That was a good thing. I collected my handbag and scarf. Dunker carried both trophies.

"When we got to the car, he popped open the rumble seat and stood the trophies in the footwell behind my seat. He flipped his palms face up, guys-only style. I slapped them hard. He hugged me tightly. I orbited."

"Let's drop the top. The night is beautiful. The sky is scattered with stars and the moon is full." Dunker said.

"He pulled the ragtop back and then opened the car door for me to get in. I was glad the seat was there, and small, too. We were almost, shoulder-to-shoulder. Dunker put his right arm around my shoulders and reached across his body with his left hand to turn the car key in the ignition. The motor gunned. Big Blue took off. I forgot to tie my scarf on properly. All the curls on the top of my head shifted. I yelled for Dunker to stop the car. He maneuvered Big Blue to the curb. Luckily, it was under a streetlight. 'What's up, Mariah?' his voice quivered.

"'My hair! My hair!' I cried.

"Tears were all over my face. I couldn't stop them. All I could think about was the time I'd spent in Miss Pearl's chair and how good I looked when I left the house. Now, it was a mess. Dunker helped to collect the bobby pins and hairpins from my lap. His fingers felt clumsy when he fiddled with my curls, trying to fix them. Afterward, I tied my scarf back on."

"Now, I understand what happened to your head."

"What do you mean?"

"Your hair. It's got a strange twist to it."

I shoved my pillows aside and dashed to the mirror.

"Yikes! No wonder I got such strange looks from Mama and Daddy when I came in the house."

"Yeah, but go on. They'll get over it."

"Sitting back down and cradling my bedding, I said, "After my hair was under control, so I thought, we went back to the 24-Hour Curb-a-Burger and had a pancake breakfast."

"You couldn't find any place else in town to eat?"

"Do you want to hear the rest of the story or not?"

"Yeah, go on."

"We left the Curb-a-Burger and headed to the park. It was so crowded Dunker had to park off the road, under a big tree. We walked uphill to the overlook. Right there under the brightness of the moon and glittering stars, Dunker stood behind me and put his hands around my waist. It felt good, but when I spoke, my head started spinning and my words sounded like gibberish."

"Were you drunk?"

"Of course not! Stop me again and you'll never . . ."

"Okay! Okay!"

"After a while, we walked back to the car. When Dunker leaned, to open the door, he kissed me."

"What did you do?"

"I don't know. Kiss him back? I think. But, for sure, I got back in the car. I don't know which took off faster, the car or my heart. We left there and went to Sly's backyard party.

"When we saw all the cars, Dunker slowed down 'til Blue stopped. With his arms around me, he pulled me toward him. He asked me something."

Delilah threw back her cover and sprang up to her knees. "Well! What did he ask you?" Her neck was stretched. She was ready to snatch every word.

"I don't remember."

"What!"

"Well. I know but I forgot. But, I do remember my lips touched his. I just don't remember if his touched mine."

"You don't remember?"

I fell over in my bed still hugging my prom dress. I pulled the covers over my head. Delilah was left hanging out of the bed with her mouth fully opened and ready to catch all the snippets of what happened next.

15

The All-night Party
Mariah

Buried beneath the covers, I skipped telling Delilah that Dunker had asked me to be his girl and to go steady with him. I had to digest that part of the story myself. Delilah will have to dream her own dreams of when she goes to her prom. Somebody might even kiss her and ask her to be their girl.

The evening was great, until Dunker and I got to the all-night party. Those words still give me a brain freeze. It was a disaster. I didn't want to tell Delilah about that, either. Dunker and I got there late because we went moon-gazing after we ate. We had to park three blocks from Sly's house. I could see the party lights in the backyard and hear the music. It seemed to drum along with my erratic heartbeat.

Sly and the Bender twins greeted Dunker and me when we strolled up the driveway leading to the rear yard.

"Come on back. Have something to eat and drink," Sly said.

The party was in full swing. The couples jammed to our dance moves. I turned to see what was happening around the yard. My eyes blinked when I saw the guys lip-locked with the girls and kissing more passionately than my parents would have approved of. My fingernails dug into my fisted hand. The other hand pressed the purse against my gut to keep down the pancakes.

Dunker and I said hello to everyone we knew and to those who weren't lip-locked, but drinking what they shouldn't be drinking and smoking cigarettes. I didn't get any closer to them than necessary. Even though Daddy had prayed for my soul, prayer or no prayer, Mama would have seared my hide, if she thought that I had a mind to drink or smoke something. I looked at Dunker and back at the dancers hanging around the garage. I tried to make small talk with one or two cheerleaders but kept getting tongue-tied. I started sweating and coming unglued. I didn't know what to do. I had already spent a good amount of the night dancing on Dunker's toes and now this.

My face grew tense and tight as I watched the couples backed up against the bushes and trees trying to merge into a single unit. Hands were researching places they should not have been, at least, according to Mama, Mrs. Donell, and my Sunday School teacher. I couldn't imagine Dunker putting his hands on me in such a way.

If Mrs. Donell were here, she'd clear out this yard with her broom-whacking moves. I saw her use them on her big boys and their cronies when they got out of line.

Finally, Dunker asked me to dance. The music was tender and wonderful, but the mood was different. Not cozy like it was at the prom.

"You're not having a good time," Dunker said.

I couldn't answer him. My feet sank into the soft ground. Fear choked me. Tears swelled behind my eyelids. I fought not to let them drop on my cheeks. I wanted to leave, but I didn't know how to say so. I didn't want to spoil Dunker's evening either.

"Excuse me, Dunker. I think I have something in my eye."

I rushed to the food table and grabbed a napkin. I dabbed at my eyes. The something that wasn't there didn't come out, instead, tears seeped out. I put my hand in my purse to make sure the dimes Mama gave me were still there. Was this the *just-in-case* moment?

Dunker came from behind and put his arm around my shoulders.

"You're shaking," he whispered. "Let's go back to the overlook. The stars are still out."

"Okay. Give me a moment to finish my drink."

I reached for Dunker's arm and held on with gratitude, but kept my chin close to my chest so he couldn't see my fright or my tears. I sipped a tropical drink until my nerves untangled themselves. When they finally did, I put the punch cup down.

Dunker and I smiled, shook hands with our friends, and said goodbye to everyone at our table. I was so glad to see Big Blue, I opened my own door. I got in and closed it on the skirt of my gown. Dunker laughed so hard his shoulders bounced up to his ears.

"Blue's got himself a pink sail ready to collect the wind."

Dunker opened the door and pushed the chiffon underneath the dashboard. He raced around the back fender and hopped over the door and dropped into the driver's seat. He settled behind the steering wheel and adjusted his high-waters. He headed Big Blue back down the road toward the park. On the way, he pulled into the 24-Hour Curb-a-Burger and ordered two cones. I couldn't stop giggling.

"You okay over there?" Dunker asked.

"Yeah."

At the overlook, we were able to park close to the observation wall and stayed in the car. We gazed out at the city lights and up at the stars. We talked about school, graduation, and our college plans. We dreamed our dreams together and solved most of the world's problems. We even wondered aloud why President Kennedy, the Prime Minister, Pope Paul, Queen Elizabeth, and the world leaders we don't know never asked teens for their advice. We decided that it was their loss and had a good chuckle.

We kissed with the taste of pineapple sherbet melting between our lips. Dunker cranked his neck. He looked at me. 'Can we go steady?' Yes, I told him, not sure if that was the right thing to say, or if I should have said more. Dunker smiled, so I guess it was okay. Now, we're boyfriend-girlfriend. Love you, Dunker, wherever you are. And I'm glad I can give Mama her dimes back.

16

Dunker's Home
Dunker

Mariah's my girl. She loves me. I'm sure she does. Her kisses were smooth and wet. Her arms held me tight, the way girls do when they like you.

"Oh, squeeze me good, Mariah!" I mumbled.

The lights in the kitchen were on. Mom and Dad were standing near the sink, talking, and sharing a bag of chips. I grabbed the back of the car seat and braced myself. With the spring of a gymnast, I was out of the car with both feet on the ground. I retrieved the trophy and headed for the kitchen door. The heels of my basketball shoes snagged Mom's mums and her sweet peas, too.

Mom's lecture struck up its usual tune in my

head. *You're in the doghouse until you fill in the gaps in my garden. You know what that means. Grab that pail of tools and get busy. Call me when you're done. In the meantime, I'll think about feeding you.*

I scraped the heel of each shoe against the steps. I pulled the screen door open to let myself in.

"Hello, dear. How was the prom?" Mom asked.

"Great."

"Don't you move! Not one inch. Take those shoes off. Park 'em outside. From the looks of your feet, you've got work to do when the sun comes up," Mom said.

After I put my shoes on the step, she offered me something to eat. But there was no way I could stomach more food. I was full of cheeseburgers, French fries, chocolate shakes, pancakes, sherbet, and Mariah.

"Mom, I can't eat now. I gotta go to bed. I'll take care of your garden when I get up. I promise."

I went straight to my room. The rustling side let me know that Toby and Paco were in the forbidden area.

"What are you doing in here? I told you to stay out of my room."

I reached for Toby's neck. He ducked, rolled off the bed, and landed on the floor gawking at me. Doesn't he know I'll pounce on him?

"I've been waiting for you, Dunker. I want to know if you danced with her. Did you hold her hand? Did you kiss her on the mouth?"

"Dance with who? Hold whose hands? Kiss who? What are you talking about?"

"You know. Mariah. Tell me. Tell me what happened at the prom."

"There's nothing to tell. Get off my universe or be buried in dog poop."

Toby took my words as an invitation to get in my face. Because he was two feet shorter than me, he had to goose-neck to make his demand. I wanted to stomp on him 'til he was nose-to-nose with Paco. He'd give him a good licking.

"Hehehe!"

"What'cha laughin' about, Dunker?"

"Beat it, Toby. Get while you can still walk."

"Okay. But just tell me, did you kiss her?"

"Sure did."

"Did she like it?"

"Yeah, all the girls like it when I kiss them."

"Did you like kissing her?"

"So much, I kissed her at least ten more times."

"Gross!"

Toby wiped his mouth with his pajama sleeve as if someone had kissed him.

"I think I'll skip the prom when I grow up. See you in the morning. I'm out of here."

Toby left the room so fast, the fish painted on his pajama pants were schooling.

I put my trophy on the chest of drawers and let my tuxedo fall to the floor. The party was over and Mariah wasn't the same person. Not the chick who played one-on-one with me or teamed with me for a pick-up game at the park. Just the way the gym was transformed into a ballroom, Mariah was transformed into a gorgeous, tall, brown lady, smooth as shaving cream, and oh, so pretty. When I put my arms around her, I could hardly dance her around the gym, and I

Judith C. Owens-Lalude

didn't mind her dirtying the toecaps of my new shoes. The lady messed with my mind and I didn't care.

Tonight, I knew I had fun. I fell in love and there's no one else in this world like Mariah. And, she's my girl now.

"Woo-wee. I love you, girl."

The weight of my body sank into the mattress. The coolness of the sheets soothed my hot damp skin and coaxed me into a dream.

Mariah and I glided across the dance floor. Turning in circles, we wrapped our bodies around each other. I gazed into her eyes. Her intense beauty made my flesh ripple. The hairs on my arms stood up. The realness of the dream woke me. I turned over but went back to sleep. *Consumed by pink clouds, I was all over Mariah and spinning her in circles. I kissed her as much as I wanted and for as long as I wanted– not letting go and not letting it end.*

The next morning, Dad knocked on the door. When he appeared from behind it, the dream vanished.

DUNKER

"You up, Dunker? It's late. How was the prom, son?"

"It was good, Dad. Mariah and I are going steady now."

"What does that mean?"

"She'll only go out with me. The guys will have to eat crow and take her off their Must-Date list."

"Sounds good. Get dressed. Mom's cooked a good breakfast. We're all waiting to hear about the prom and the trophy you brought home."

I snatched my bathrobe from the hook on the back of the bedroom door and went downstairs for breakfast and the intense interview.

"Good morning, son. You look different."

"He's in love, honey."

Dad winked at Mom and sat down.

"Is it that girl you took to the Prom last night?" Grandma asked.

"Un hun," I said.

"I think you've been bitten by the love bug," Grandma said.

Toby picked up his fork. He opened his mouth

to say something, but I put my hand up. He grinned, backed down, and ate his grits. Nothing more was said until the telephone rang.

The End

Discussion Questions

1) What kind of person was Dunker?

2) What was it about Dunker that would have made him a better team captain than Sly?

3) Were Dunker's teammates always fair to him?

4) Why didn't Dunker's mother want him to get a shave?

6) Describe Dunker's barbershop experience.

7) How was Dunker's relationship with his basketball, car, and teammates similar?

8) Describe Dunker's relationship with his father?

9) Did Mariah intentionally avoid Dunker when he first tried to ask her for a date? If so, why.

10) How did Toby and Delilah's characters add to the story?

11). Describe the relationships Toby and Delilah had with Dunker and Mariah.

12) What were the challenges Dunker encountered when he tried to ask Mariah to go to the prom with him?

13) What would you have done differently to get a prom date with Mariah?

14) Why was Mr. Drew, Dunker's Physics teacher, hard on him?

15) What were the similarities between Dunker's family and Mariah's family?

16) Describe how Mariah's mother treated Delilah when Mariah was preparing for the prom?

17) Why was Mariah right not to tell Delilah everything that happened prom night?

18) At what point in the story did you think Mariah might have to use the coins in her purse?

19) Was the party after the prom the type you would like to go to? If so, why? If not, why not?

20) What was it about Dunker's behavior that let readers know that Mariah was special to him?

21). Describe the relationship between Dunker and Big Blue.

22) How were Dunker's and Mariah's families similar or different from yours?

23) Did Dunker's Grandmother add to the story or was she a distraction? Defend your point of view.

24) What happened after Dunker and Mariah graduated from high School college?

Photographs from Judith C. Owens-Lalude's
1965 High School Photo Album

Judith, Center, Cheerleader Captain
1965 Louisville, kY, Central High School

Judith, 1965 Kentucky
All-Star Cheerleader

Judith, third from the right, 1965 Kentucky All-Star Cheerleaders,
Courier-Journal, Staff Photo, June 1965

Judith , 1965 Pink Prom Gown

About the Author

Judith C. Owens-Lalude grew up in Louisville, Kentucky. As a young girl she loved sports. Because both her parents were accomplished in aquatics, her first real sport was swimming. If asked, she would say, "I don't remember when I couldn't swim." As a middle schooler, tennis and swimming were her summer sports. Basketball was added as her middle school, winter sport. During her freshman year at Central High School, in Louisville, Kentucky, she became a member of the tennis team and varsity cheerleading squad. Owens-Lalude was the squad's captain her senior year. That summer she made the Kentucky All Star Cheerleading squad.

Owens-Lalude of Louisville Central High School was a 1965 Kentucky-Indiana All-Star Cheerleader. Alfred "Butch" Beard, from Breckenridge County High School in Hardinsburg, Kentucky, was **Kentucky Mr. Basketball 1965.** He played on the 1965 Kentucky-Indiana All-Star Basketball team. Judith was assigned to jump for "Butch" when his name was announced.

Butch Beard,
Kentucky Mr. Basketball 1965

A special thanks to Alfred Beard for allowing his image to be used to help tell the story of high school basketball, romances, and a prom.

Little did they know at that moment, 2016, that 51 years later they would reconnect in Louisville, Kentucky.

Alfred "Butch" Beard, Jr., of Hardinsburg, Kentucky,  was 6' 3", 185 pounds; a Point Guard for the University of Louisville basketball team; and was selected by the Atlanta Hawks of the National Basketball Association (NBA) in the 1st round of the 1969 draft. He also played professional basketball and later coached for the NBA. In the Fall of 2015, he returned to Louisville, Kentucky to coach the Women's Basketball Team of Simmons College of Kentucky.

Alfred "Butch" Beard read *DUNKER*. He remarked, "Judith, you hit the jackpot! Thank you for taking us back to the 60s to our high school prom. Dunker and Mariah were very emotional, it brought back a flood of memories. The book is a super read. One would say *DUNKER* is a slam dunk!"

Other books

by Judith C. Owens-Lalude:

PICKIN"

Peas and the Popover

BOO! That's My Pumpkin

BOO! THAT'S MY PUMPKIN Coloring Book

Donavan's Boots and Blisters

Kaleidoscope Kids

Kaleidoscope Kids Coloring Book

Kaleidoscope Kids Balloons Coloring Book

The Midnight Boy from South Sudan

Wedding Drums and the Tall-Tall Tree

Miss Lucy: Slave and Civil War Nurse

The Long Walk: Slavery to Freedom

Bloody Trails: Enslavement & Freedom

www.ingramcontent.com/pod-product-compliance
Lightning Source LLC
Chambersburg PA
CBHW061636040426
42446CB00010B/1448